AN ATLAS OF TOLKIEN

To my father, Alan Day

Thunder Bay Press
An imprint of Printers Row Publishing Group
9717 Pacific Heights Blvd, San Diego, CA 92121
www.thunderbaybooks.com • mail@thunderbaybooks.com

Artwork, design & layout copyright © Octopus Publishing Group 2024
Text copyright © David Day 2015, 2019, 2024

Some or all of the material in this book originally appeared in *A Tolkien Bestiary* and/or *The Tolkien Encyclopaedia* and/or *The World of Tolkien*, published by Octopus Publishing Group, 1979, 1991, 1993, 2003

Printers Row Publishing Group is a division of Readerlink Distribution Services, LLC.
Thunder Bay Press is a registered trademark of Readerlink Distribution Services, LLC.

Correspondence regarding the content of this book should be sent to Thunder Bay Press, Editorial Department, at the above address. Author inquiries should be addressed to Pyramid, an imprint of Octopus Publishing Group Ltd., Carmelite House, 50 Victoria Embankment, London, EC4Y 0DZ, www.octopusbooks.co.uk

THUNDER BAY PRESS
Publisher: Peter Norton
Associate Publisher: Ana Parker
Editor: Dan Mansfield

PYRAMID
Publisher: Lucy Pessell
Designer: Isobel Platt
Editor: Feyi Oyesanya
Assistant Editor: Samina Rahman
Production Manager: Peter Hunt
Cover Illustration: Ian Miller

For illustration credits, refer to page 9

Library of Congress Control Number: 2024931337

ISBN: 978-1-6672-0773-5

Printed in China
28 27 26 25 24   1 2 3 4 5

AN ATLAS OF TOLKIEN

David Day

THUNDER BAY
P·R·E·S·S

San Diego, California

Gandalf and Shadowfax

A NOTE ON THIS EDITION

An *Atlas of Tolkien* (2015) was created as a geographical and chronological guide for readers of *The Hobbit* and *The Lord of the Rings* who wished to know more of the vast imaginary world in which these books are set. It was also meant as a useful compass to encourage those who wish to navigate the somewhat deeper waters of *The Silmarillion* and Tolkien's many other posthumously published texts.

Its conception was due to the vision and persistence of Samantha Warrington and Anna Bowles and is a compilation of specially commissioned and created art from some of the most talented fantasy artists of the past four decades.

It all began with the enormous investment in original art exclusively commissioned for the publication of *A Tolkien Bestiary* (1979) as the first ever fully illustrated reference work on J. R. R. Tolkien. *A Tolkien Bestiary* appeared just two years after the posthumous publication of J. R. R. Tolkien's *The Silmarillion*: a book that for the first time gave readers of *The Hobbit* and *The Lord of the Rings* some indication of the immense scope of Tolkien's mythology and cosmology. Subsequently, new original artwork was created for *Tolkien: The Illustrated Encyclopedia* (1992), and for *The World of Tolkien: The Mythological Sources of Lord of the Rings* (2002).

An Atlas of Tolkien and its companion volume, *A Dictionary of Tolkien,* were the first two books of a seven-volume reference library that comprises *The Battles of Tolkien* (2016), *The Heroes of Tolkien* (2017), *The Dark Powers of Tolkien* (2018), *The Hobbits of Tolkien* (1993, 2019) and *The Ring Legends of Tolkien* (1994, 2020). This series includes further research and study, as well as work from a new generation of talented artists.

This special edition of *An Atlas of Tolkien* has been expanded to include that more recent study, and a selection of work from some of the many artists who have contributed to the books published within the past decade, including *The Illustrated World of Tolkien* (2019) and *The Illustrated World of Tolkien: The Second Age* (2023), which delves into the lesser-known parts of Tolkien's legendarium. It publishes alongside a special edition of *A Dictionary of Tolkien*.

CONTENTS

ACKNOWLEDGEMENTS

Artworks and illustrations have been supplied by the following artists:

Ivan Allen: 8
Victor Ambrus: 4, 153, 208
Graham Bence: 219, 222-223
John Blanche: 110-111, 114-115, 147, 178-179
Jaroslav Bradac: 35, 139
Rachel Chilton: 194-195, 215
Tim Clarey: 160, 164, 172, 185, 198
Alan Curless: 18-19, 156-157, 174-175, 186-187, 228, 238-239
Sally Davies: 14-15, 22-23, 30, 36, 48, 55, 76, 91, 96, 118, 121, 137, 144, 243
Michael Foreman: 50-51, 64, 67, 80-81, 95, 165, 214, 245
Linda Garland: 44-45, 62-63, 92-93
Melvin Grant: 84, 189, 220, 225, 237
Sam Hadley: 74, 162, 232
David Kearney: 141, 176, 186, 200
Pauline Martin: 29, 60, 170, 200
Mauro Mazzarra: 104-105, 124, 130-131
Ian Miller: 70-71, 83, 87, 192, 206-207, 210-211, 230-231
Andrew Mockett: 73, 201
Turner Mohan: 90
Lidia Postma: 107, 217, 246
Peter Price: 127, 155, 163, 197
Kip Rasmussen: 33, 109, 113, 134
David Roberts: 85, 86, 169
Šárka Škorpíková: 10-11, 42, 98, 161
Jamie Whyte: 53, 56-57, 120, 166-167, 182-183, 184, 202-203, 212-213, 226-227

Ossiríand

PREFACE

The aim of this *Atlas* is to reveal something of the imaginative sweep and splendour of Tolkien's epic world. It is a vehicle of entry into – and travel through – the complex geography and mythology of Middle-earth and the Undying Lands.

Time is as essential to the mapping of Middle-earth as geographic location. This *Atlas* gives a chronological context for events because in Tolkien's world maps are only valid if they are located in time as well as place. His world of Middle-earth and the Undying Lands constantly evolves through time.

However, let us make clear just what this *Atlas* is – and what it is not.

An atlas, traditionally, is a book of maps, tables, charts, and illustrations about a specific place or subject. Often it is a road map and illustrated guide for anything from the geography of the world to the anatomy of the human body.

This *Atlas* will give a geographic and chronological context for the narratives of *The Hobbit, The Lord of the Rings,* and *The Silmarillion*, but it will not offer the narratives themselves. For that, one must go to the actual novels.

This *Atlas* locates and illustrates the fair Lúthien Tinúviel singing before the iron crown of Morgoth in the Quest of the Silmaril in the First Age. You will discover where and when in the Third Age, Bilbo Baggins encounters Smaug the Dragon in the Quest of Lonely Mountain. During the Quest of the Ring, you will also learn where – and in which crucial battle – the Witch-king and the Shield-maiden are locked in combat.

However, the *Atlas* will not tell you what happened after Lúthien stopped singing, or how Bilbo fared in his contest with the Dragon. Nor does it reveal who won the duel between the Witch-king and the Shield-maiden.

The *Atlas* is intentionally full of cliff-hangers. It is not – nor is it intended to be – a substitute for reading the actual stories in *The Hobbit, The Lord of the Rings,* or *The Silmarillion*. If you haven't already read the books, you will have the pleasure of discovering what happened next when you do read them.

Throughout the *Atlas*, the outcomes of events and battles are only told if their results relate to the geographical evolution of Arda. The reader will find the *Atlas* is a useful compass in the exploration of Tolkien's world, and it will give a sense of the deep history that motivates actions and deeds – for both good and evil – in all his characters.

With this *Atlas*, you won't need to be an expert in Elvish to find your way around Middle-earth and the Undying Lands. It has been written and organized in a way that is both informative and accessible to the general reader. The book is mostly written for those who have read at least one of the books – or have seen the movies, and would wish to read the books. Or, more commonly, for someone who, having read one book, might wish to have a guide to make the transition to the next book. One reason for the sustained fascination with Tolkien's novels is to be found in the complex and detailed cosmology behind the stories. However, the cosmology is also one of the obstacles to understanding certain basic ideas in his creation of Middle-earth. In fact, many of these obstacles are geographic and cosmological in nature, and our hope is that some obstacles may be resolved by the overall view provided by this *Atlas*.

In the 1950s, in one of his letters, J. R. R. Tolkien acknowledged that the location of his world often confused people, and he stated: 'Many reviewers seem to assume that Middle-earth is another planet!' He found that a perplexing conclusion. In his own mind, he had not the least doubt about its locality: 'Middle-earth is not an imaginary world. The name is the modern form of midden-erd>middle-erd, an ancient name for the oikoumene, the abiding place of Men, the objectively real world, in use specifically opposed to imaginary worlds (as Fairyland) or unseen worlds (as Heaven and Hell)'.

A decade later, Tolkien gave a journalist a more exact location: 'the action of the story takes place in the North-west of Middle-earth, equivalent in latitude to the coastline of Europe and the north shore of the Mediterranean … If Hobbiton and Rivendell are taken (as intended) to be about the latitude of Oxford, then Minas Tirith, 600 miles south, is at about the latitude of Florence. The Mouths of the Anduin and the ancient city of Pelargir are at about the latitude of ancient Troy'.

The trick of Tolkien's world is not so much the *where*, but the *when*: 'The theatre of my tale is this earth, the one in which we now live, but the historical period is imaginary'. And in another letter: 'I have, I suppose, constructed an imaginary time, but kept my feet on my own mother-earth for place'.

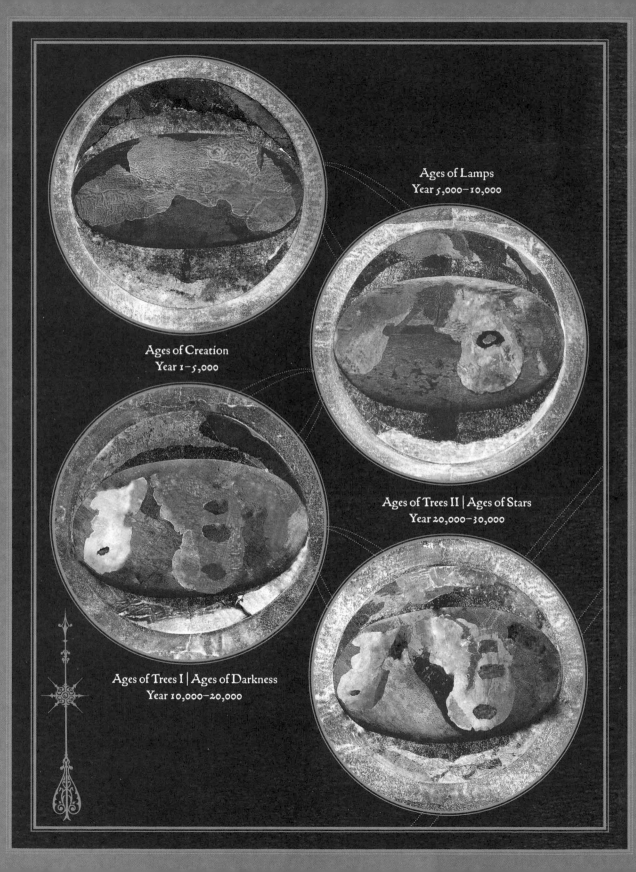

Ages of Lamps
Year 5,000–10,000

Ages of Creation
Year 1–5,000

Ages of Trees II | Ages of Stars
Year 20,000–30,000

Ages of Trees I | Ages of Darkness
Year 10,000–20,000

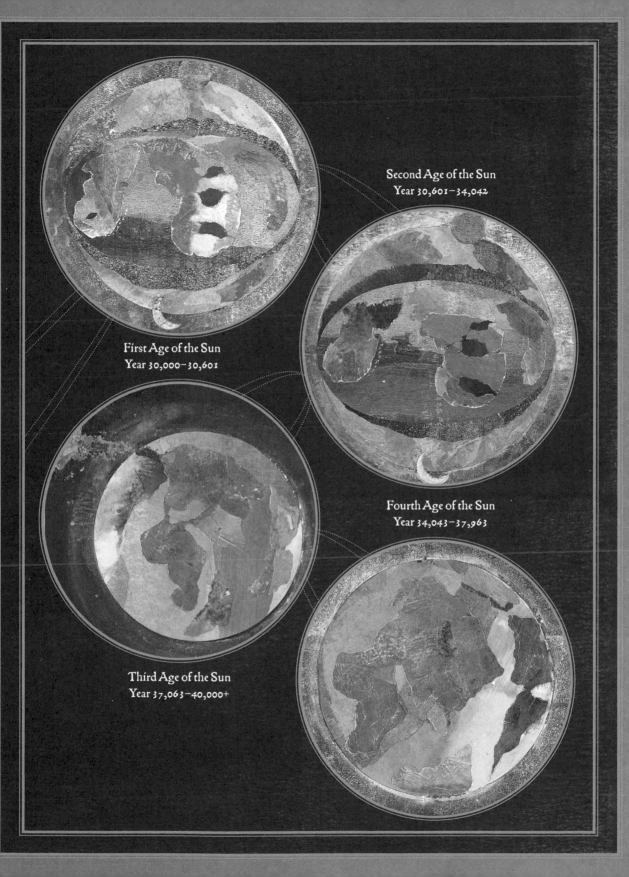

Second Age of the Sun
Year 30,601–34,042

First Age of the Sun
Year 30,000–30,601

Fourth Age of the Sun
Year 34,043–37,963

Third Age of the Sun
Year 37,063–40,000+

That imaginary time is a mythical one, just before the first recorded human histories and the rise of any recorded historic civilization. It begins with a new creation myth which results in the making of a flat planet within spheres of air and light. It is inhabited by the godlike Valar, and eventually Elves, Dwarves, Ents and Orcs. According to Tolkien's own reckoning (in his *Earliest Annals of Valimar)*, we are 30,000 years into the history of this world before the human race appears. Another 3,900 years pass before the cataclysmic destruction of the Atlantis-like culture of Númenor, resulting in this mythical world's transformation into the globed world we know today. The events of the remaining 4,000 years of Tolkien's annals were then intended to lead 'eventually and inevitably to ordinary history'. Tolkien was consciously inventing a cosmology comparable to the Norse, Greek, Finnish, German and Celtic traditions. The enormity of this undertaking is staggering. It would be as if Homer, before writing the *Iliad* and the *Odyssey*, had first to invent the whole of Greek mythology and history. What is most remarkable is that Tolkien actually achieved his ambitions to an extraordinary degree.

The mapping of Tolkien's world through time presents a considerable challenge that is complicated by a number of quite unique problems. Although Arda is almost a biblical creationist world that does not entertain the idea of Darwinian evolution, it is definitely a world that embraces the ideas of Charles Lyle's geological evolution – and the later theory of continental drift – with a vengeance. The movement of continents in our primary (real) world took place over hundreds of millions of years; in Tolkien's world their movement takes place in the relatively rapid measure of many thousands of years.

Still, the mapping of Middle-earth and the Undying Lands requires the charting of a shifting geography over tens of thousands of years. Accepting this, the task of this *Atlas* was to discover a way to present the evolution of Tolkien's world coherently in texts, maps and illustrations. This task was not made easier by the fact that there are aspects of Tolkien's world that are incomplete, inconsistent and at times self-contradictory. Indeed, Christopher Tolkien, in his editing of *The Shaping of Middle-earth*, observed that although geographical and chronological concerns became a central preoccupation in his work, his father ultimately 'never achieved a complete and coherent structure'.

However, the incompleteness, inconsistency and self-contradictory aspects of the Norse and Icelandic mythology, for instance, have not been an obstacle to the many speculative reconstructions of the world of the Scandinavian gods. And just as there have been many manuals, guides and maps of ancient Greek, Egyptian and Babylonian cosmologies, so here with *An Atlas of Tolkien* we have created a geographic and chronological guide to Middle-earth and the Undying Lands.

Any such undertaking, of course, should require a warning that to greater and lesser degrees, there is an aspect of subjective interpretation involved. We are not dealing with the laws of physics here, but an imaginary literary world. J. R. R. Tolkien gives numerous systems of measuring time and several hand-sketched maps of Arda in the posthumous *The Shaping of Middle-earth* that are not consistent with those in *The Silmarillion* and *The Lord of the Rings*. In this *Atlas*, we have taken as many clues as we can from his writing to give a consistent overview of the geographic and historic evolution from the creation of his world to the time of the War of the Ring.

To clarify, and give a framework for understanding the vast stretches of time that preceded the events of *The Hobbit* and *The Lord of the Rings,* as well as giving them a historic and geographic context, I have chosen to adopt a convention not actually used by Tolkien and speak of the 'Ages of the Sun'. This is to differentiate systems of time and place (at times these systems overlap) before the appearance of the sun in the heavens. These vast passages of time before the rising of the sun, I have similarly called: 'Ages of Creation', 'Ages of the Lamps of the Valar', 'Ages of the Trees of Light', 'Ages of Darkness' and 'Ages of the Stars'.

These ages are fairly consistent with Tolkien in his earliest annals account: 'the First Ages of the World were ended and these are reckoned as 30,000 years or 3,000 years of the Valar'. And after the rising of the sun, he observes: 'from this time are reckoned the years of the Sun … And after came measured time into the World'.

In the years just before the publication of *The Lord of the Rings*, Tolkien wrote that – in his most extravagant imaginings – he hoped others might involve themselves in his world: 'I would draw some of the great tales in fullness, and leave many only placed in the scheme, and sketched. These cycles should be linked to a majestic whole, and yet leave scope for other minds and hands, wielding paint and music and drama'.

Once again, Tolkien achieved those aims to an extraordinary degree: many 'other minds and hands' have subsequently been at work. His writing has inspired artists, musicians and dramatic renderings. And as can be observed in this *Atlas*, Tolkien has certainly inspired the artists 'wielding paint' who place his tales in a context 'linked to a majestic whole'.

EKKAIA – The Encircling Sea

AMAN

Trees of the Valar

Mansions of Manwë and Varda

Taniquetil

HELCARAXË

The Grinding Ice

Pelóri Mountains

Ring of Doom

Valimar

Formenos

Tirion

Pass of Light

VALINOR

ELDAMAR

Halls of Nienna

Mansions of Aulë

Halls of Mandos

Isle of Estë

Lake of Lórellin

Gardens of Lórien

UNDYING LANDS

Pelóri Mountains

Woods of Orome

Avathar

Pastures of Yavanna

Hyarmentir

Pelóri Mountains

Aqualondë

Bay of Eldamar

TOL ERESSËA

Avallonë

ENCHANTED ISLES

Shadowy Seas

Andunië

Romenna

Armenelos

NUMENOR

BELEGAER

The Great

A COMPOSITE
MAP OF ARDA

Published nearly five decades ago, the beautifully rendered map on the previous pages is something of an historical artifact. It was the first map to attempt to chart Tolkien's whole world of Arda. And if one keeps in mind the composite nature of this map of Tolkien's world 'through the ages'; it may still serve as a useful compass for Tolkien readers who wish to speculate on the location of Arda's many long vanished realms.

Before this map appeared in *A Tolkien Bestiary* in 1979, there were essentially only two published maps of Middle-earth: one in *The Lord of the Rings* in 1955 and one in *The Silmarillion* in 1977. The area of these two maps in the context of Arda would be comparable to the size of western Europe in a map of the world. And there were no maps that revealed anything of the geography of the rest of Tolkien's Middle-earth, or anything at all of the Undying Lands, or the seas about them.

It would be impossible in a single map to accurately show the many massive shifts of the landmasses that transformed Arda over thirty-seven millennia: a task made even more challenging by its transition from a flat world to a globed sphere. However, we wished to give readers an elementary sense of geographic orientation when texts referred to such places as: Almaren, the island of the Valar in the time of the Great Lamps, or the Trees of Light in Valinor, or the Dungeons of Utumno in the Ages of Darkness, or the shores of the Inland Sea of Helcar where the Elves were awakened by starlight, or Hildórien where Men came into existence with the world's first sunrise.

To clarify the purpose of this map, the Introduction to *A Tolkien Bestiary* gives the proviso that it is 'an original interpretation from Tolkien's writings and should be used only for general orientation. It shows all the lands of Arda, even though many of them, as well as many of the great realms, did not exist at the same time, in fact, much of Arda seems to have vanished completely by the time of the War of the Ring'.

The shifting geography from age to age sometimes presented logistical problems. Tolkien's two maps were both roughly in the same region of the northwest of Middle-earth, but by the time of *The Lord of the Rings*, the earlier land of Beleriand had sunk beneath the sea. So, in order to include the shorelines of both those maps in this composite rendering, Beleriand was lifted from the sea bed and placed just north of the landmass appearing in *The Lord of the Rings* map of Middle-earth. Similarly, the sunken island kingdom of Númenor was also raised from the depths of the western sea of Belegaer, although its pentagon-star shape was not revealed until after the publication of *Bestiary*. All the lands that were written about in the text of *The Silmarillion* since Arda's creation were placed in a single map to give readers a general sense of the geographic orientation of those lands relative to those revealed in Tolkien's *Lord of the Rings* map. But of course, the actual shape of those landmasses and their coastlines were and remain a matter of speculation.

The mapping of Tolkien's world has only been slowly and fragmentarily revealed to its readers over many decades. It was only after the 1986 publication of Tolkien's *The Shaping of Middle-earth* that there was sufficient evidence to attempt to map out the slow evolution of Arda from the flat world of myth through the ages to a globed world within our solar system. And based on this evidence, the eight evolutionary maps of the ages of Arda were created and form the visual time-line of this Atlas.

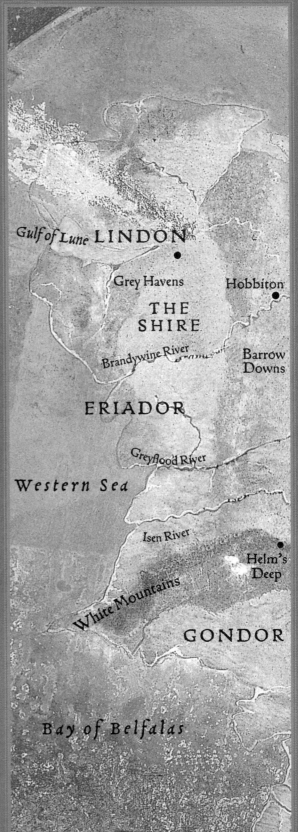

Gulf of Lune LINDON

Grey Havens

Hobbiton

THE
SHIRE

Brandywine River

Barrow
Downs

ERIADOR

Greyflood River

Western Sea

Isen River

Helm's
Deep

White Mountains

GONDOR

Bay of Belfalas

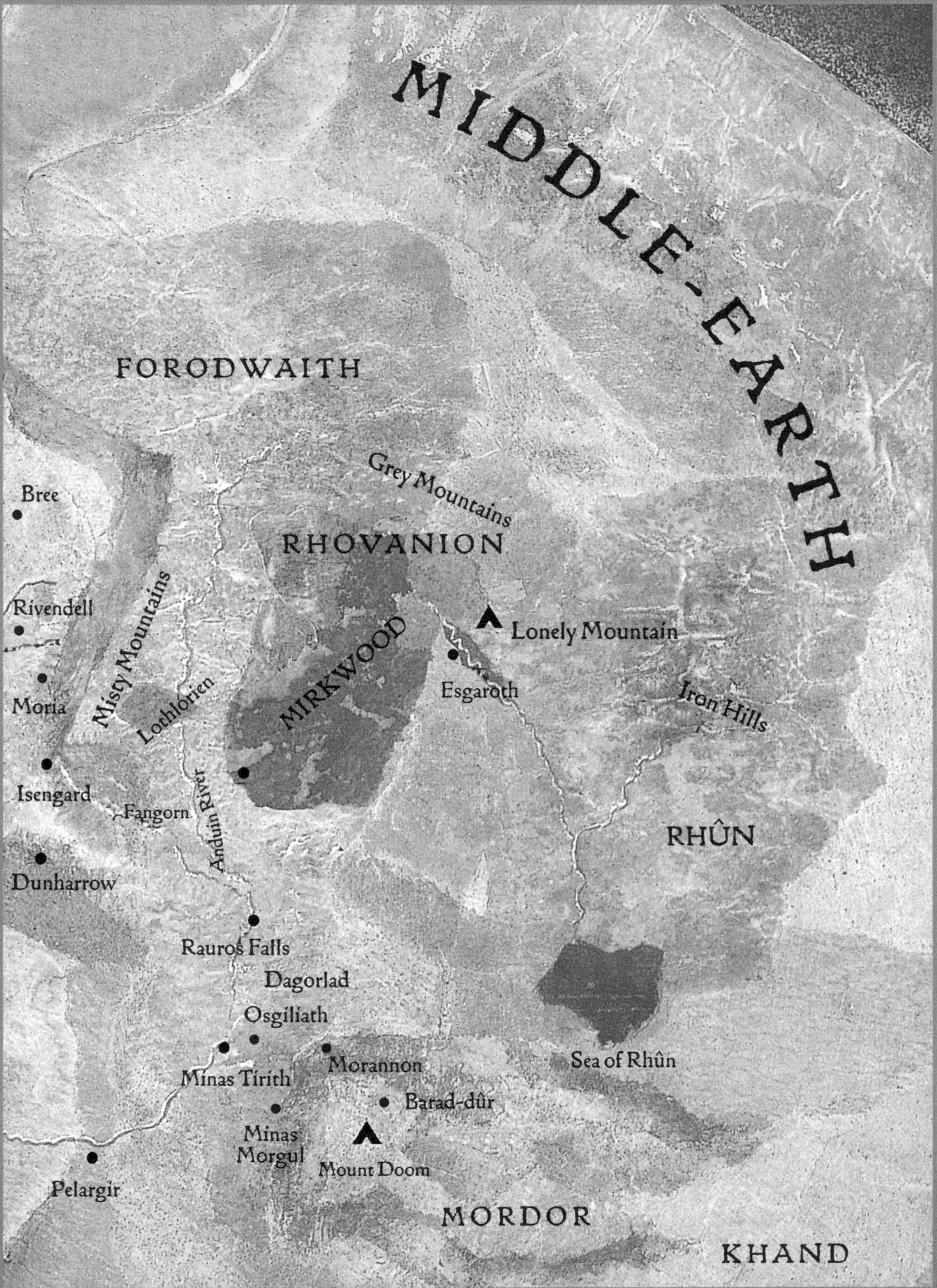

MIDDLE-EARTH

FORODWAITH

Grey Mountains

RHOVANION

Bree

Rivendell

Misty Mountains

MIRKWOOD

Lonely Mountain

Moria

Lothlórien

Esgaroth

Iron Hills

Isengard

Fangorn

Anduin River

RHÛN

Dunharrow

Rauros Falls

Dagorlad

Osgiliath

Sea of Rhûn

Morannon

Minas Tirith

Barad-dûr

Minas Morgul

Mount Doom

Pelargir

MORDOR

KHAND

A CHRONOLOGY OF MIDDLE-EARTH AND THE UNDYING LANDS

CREATION

Eru the One ('He that is Alone') * Timeless Halls fashioned * Ainur create Music of the Ainur * Vision of Eä * Creation of the World (Arda)

YEAR 1 – 1ST VALARIAN AGE

Valar and Maiar enter Arda * Arda shaped * First War * Arda marred * Melkor expelled

THE SHAPING OF ARDA

YEAR 5,000 – 5TH VALARIAN AGE

AGES OF THE LAMPS

Lamps of the Valar forged * Spring of Arda begins * Valar found Almaren * Great Forests of Arda grow * Melkor founds Utumno * Rebel Maiar enter Arda * Lamps and Almaren destroyed * Spring of Arda ends

YEAR 10,000 – 10TH VALARIAN AGE

THE UNDYING LANDS

AGES OF THE TREES

Years of Bliss * Valinor founded * City of Valimar founded * Trees of the Valar created * Eagles conceived by Manwë * Varda gathers light for Stars * Oromë reports awakening of Elves * Melian departs to Middle-earth * Valar depart for War of Powers * Chaining of Melkor * Peace of Arda begins * Summons of the Valar * Vanyar and Noldor settle in Eldamar * City of Tirion founded * Teleri arrive on Tol Eressëa * Teleri build first ships * Haven of Alqualondë founded * Noldor forge Elven jewels * Silmarils forged * Melkor unchained * Peace of Arda ends * Trees of the Valar destroyed * First Kinslaying of Elves * Flight of the Noldor

MIDDLE-EARTH

AGES OF DARKNESS

Melkor in Utumno * Melkor Lord of Middle-earth * Sleep of Yavanna begins * Melkor builds Angband * Balrogs and Great Spiders appear * Werewolves and Vampires appear * Dwarves conceived by Aulë * Yavanna visits Middle-earth * Ents conceived by Yavanna * Oromë visits Middle-earth

YEAR 20,000 – 20TH VALARIAN AGE

AGES OF STARS

Varda rekindles Stars * Elves awakened * Ents awakened * Dwarves awakened * Orcs bred in Angband * Trolls bred * Dwarves found Khazad-dum * Great Journey of Elves begins * Melian the Maia in Beleriand * Great Journey of Elves ends * Dwarves found Nogrod * Dwarves found Belegost * Sindar found Doriath * Sindar delve Menegroth * Laiquendi enter Ossiriand

YEAR 30,000 — 30TH VALARIAN AGE

FIRST AGE OF THE SUN

Moon and Sun fashioned by Valar * Melian the Maia returns to Valinor * Eärendil's pleas to the Valar * Valar depart for War of Wrath * Melkor/Morgoth expelled

Moon and Sun first appear * Men awaken in East * War of the Jewels begins * Men appear in Beleriand * Dragons bred in Angband * Noldor kingdoms destroyed * Sindar kingdoms destroyed * War of Wrath and Great Battle * Morgoth cast into the Void

YEAR 30,600 — 31ST VALARIAN AGE

SECOND AGE OF THE SUN

Avallónë founded * Valar create Númenor * Ban of the Valar * Númenor–Elves alliance * Gift of Palantíri to Númenor * Númenórean armada * Destruction of Númenor * Change of the World

Gil-galad founds Lindon * Círdan founds Grey Havens * Edain arrive in Númenor * Sauron established in Mordor * Elven-smiths found Eregion * The One Ring is forged * War of Sauron and the Elves * Eregion destroyed * Refuge of Rivendell secured * Nazgûl Ringwraiths appear * Downfall of Númenor * Last Alliance of Elves and Men * Defeat of Sauron and Mordor

YEAR 34,000 — 34TH VALARIAN AGE

THIRD AGE OF THE SUN

Long peace of Valinor begins * Istari chosen from Maia * Istari depart for Middle-earth * Eldar ships carrying the Elves of Lothlórien arrive * Eldar ships carrying the Elves of Dol Amroth arrive * Valar reject Sauron's spirit * Ringbearers' ships arrive

The One Ring lost * Easterling invasions begin * Sauron the Necromancer reappears * Hobbits first recorded in histories * Witch-king in Angmar * Great Plague * End of North Kingdom of Arnor * Balrog appears in Moria * The One Ring found * Uruk-hai and Olog-hai bred * Dragons reappear in north * War of Dwarves and Orcs * Death of Smaug the Golden * War of the Ring * Sauron's final defeat * Ringbearers' Ships sail west

YEAR 37,000 — 37TH VALARIAN AGE

FOURTH AGE OF THE SUN

Last Eldar Ship arrives

Dominion of Men begins * Last Elven Ship sails west

THE CREATION OF ARDA

THE VISION AND CREATION OF ARDA

In the beginning, the great spirits called the Ainur were bidden by Eru, the One, to create a Great Music, and out of the music came a vision like a globed light in the Void. Eru Ilúvatar gave this vision life, and it became Eä, the 'World That Is'. The Ainur looked on it and were amazed and many, for love of this new place, entered it. They became the powers that were named the Valar and the Maiar; Men later thought of them as gods. These were the beings that shaped the World, which was called Arda. Into Arda the Valar and Maiar brought many things of beauty, but also there was strife: one of the mightiest among them rebelled against Ilúvatar and his brethren and there was war.

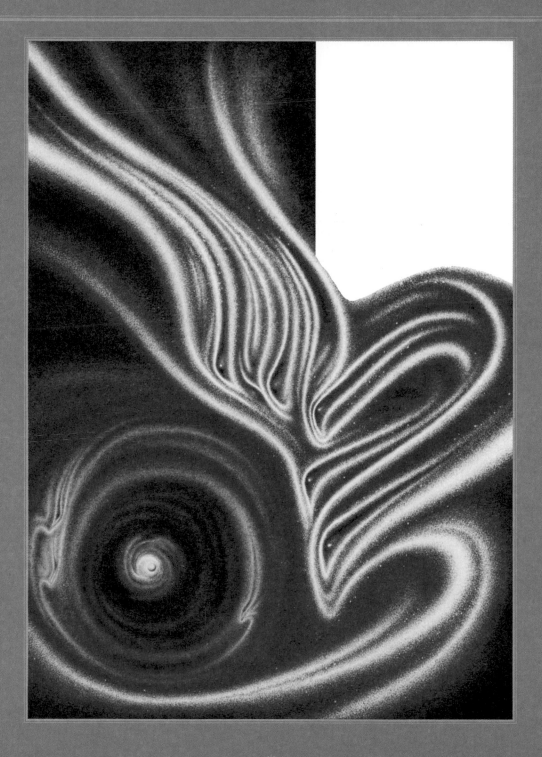

Arda is formed amid the Timeless Halls.

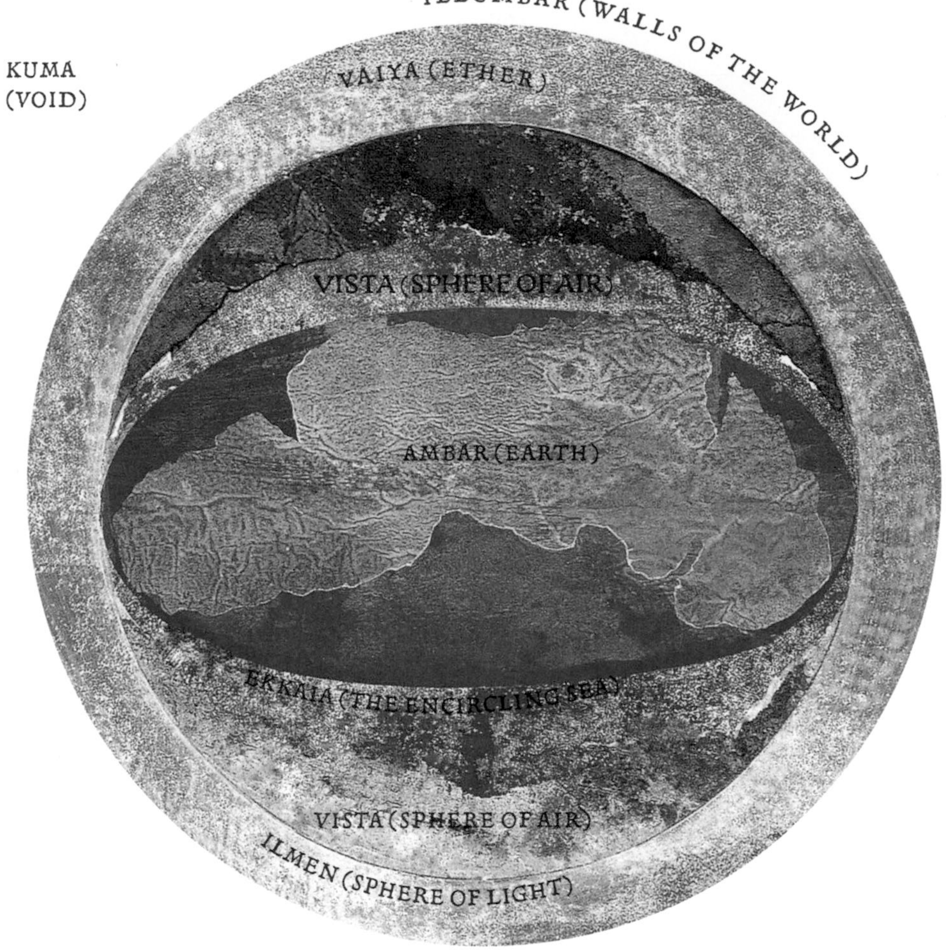

ILLUMBAR (WALLS OF THE WORLD)

KUMA (VOID)

VAIYA (ETHER)

VISTA (SPHERE OF AIR)

AMBAR (EARTH)

EKKAIA (THE ENCIRCLING SEA)

VISTA (SPHERE OF AIR)

ILMEN (SPHERE OF LIGHT)

Years 1–5,000

THE BEGINNING OF THE WORLD

When Arda was first created, the earth was a flat disc enclosed within spheres of air, light and ether. These spheres were sealed within the invisible Walls of the World, and set in the infinite Void. There was one vast supercontinent upon which the Valar, or Powers of Arda, continued the shaping of the world. But one of the Valar revolted and this led to the First War. In the conflict the ideal symmetry of Arda was ruined, and the continent was broken apart

THE AINUR

When all was darkness and a great void, according to the 'Ainulindalë', that first book of *The Silmarillion*, there was an omniscient Being who lived alone in the vast emptiness. He was called Eru, the One, or as the Elves would later name him, Ilúvatar.

This was the Being that Tolkien conceived as the source of all creation. Through the 'Ainulindalë', Tolkien tells us how the elemental thoughts of Ilúvatar became the race of gods called the Ainur (the 'Holy Ones'), and through the power of His spirit – the 'Flame Imperishable' – Ilúvatar gave the Ainur eternal life.

For this race of gods, Ilúvatar built a dwelling place in the Void, called the Timeless Halls. Here, the Ainur were taught to sing by Ilúvatar and became a vast heavenly choir. Out of the music of these god-like spirits came a holy vision that was a globed world whirling in the Void.

Tolkien's world of Arda was literally sung into being, and each of the heavenly hosts had a part in its conception, even that one mighty satanic spirit called Melkor who sang of strife and discord. However, the Music of the Ainur simply created a vision; it took the power of the Flame Imperishable to make Eä, the World That Is. Thus, the vision was given substance and reality. And into that world descended those of the Ainur who had the greatest part in its conception and who wished to take a further part in its shaping.

This was how Tolkien chronicled the creation of Arda. It is both strangely ethereal and vastly operatic in its conception. Also, it is a kind of double creation, for when the Ainur arrived on Arda, they found it was up to them to shape it.

Although Tolkien tells us that the majority of the Ainur remained with Ilúvatar in the Timeless Halls, he tells us nothing more of them. His histories deal only with those who entered the spheres of the world. Here these godly, bodiless spirits take on more physical manifestations. They become the elements and the powers of nature, but like the Greek or Norse gods they have physical form, personality, gender and kinship with one another. The Ainur who entered Arda are divided into two orders: the Valar and the Maiar – the gods and the demigods.

✳

Arda was sung into being, and each of the heavenly
hosts had a part in its conception.

THE VALAR AND THE MAIAR

The Valar numbered fifteen: Manwë, King of the Winds; Varda, Queen of the Stars; Ulmo, Lord of the Oceans; Nienna, the Weeper; Yavanna, the Fruitful; Aulë, the Smith; Oromë, Lord of Forests; Vána, the Youthful; Mandos, Keeper of the Dead; Vairë, the Weaver; Lórien, Master of Dreams; Estë, the Healer; Tulkas, the Wrestler; Nessa, the Dancer; and Melkor, who was later named Morgoth, the Dark Enemy.

Of the Maiar, there were a multitude, but only a few of these immortals are named in Tolkien's chronicles. Eönwë, Herald of Manwë; Ilmarë, Maid of Varda; Ossë of the Waves; Uinen of the Calm Seas; Melian, Queen of the Sindar; Arien, the Sun; Tilion, the Moon; Sauron, the Ring Lord; Gothmog, Lord of the Balrogs; Thuringwethil, the Vampire; Ungoliant, the Spider; Draugluin, the Werewolf; Goldberry, the River-daughter; Iarwain Ben-adar (Tom Bombadil); and the five wizards – Olórin (Gandalf); Curunír (Saruman); Aiwendil (Radagast); Alatar; and Pallando.

THE VALARIAN AGES

It is only after the world came into being and the Ainur enter into it that the count of time upon Arda begins. For the greater part of Arda's history there was no sun or moon by which to measure time, so Tolkien gives us the chronological measure of Valarian Years, and Valarian Ages. Each Valarian Year, Tolkien tells us, is equivalent to ten years as we know them. And as each Valarian Age contains a hundred Valarian Years, each Age is equivalent to one thousand mortal years. Although there are many overlapping systems and variations in events and dates in Tolkien's writings, there is enough consistency to estimate with some precision that the time elapsing from the Creation of Arda to the end of the Third Age of the Sun (shortly after the War of the Ring) was thirty-seven Valarian Ages, or more exactly 37,063 mortal years.

Within this vast time frame, the first Valarian Ages were spent by the newly arrived powers in the Shaping of Arda. However, even as there was discord in the Music of the Ainur, so when the actual Shaping of Arda began, a host of Maiar spirits, led by that mighty Vala called Melkor, created a great conflict. This was the First War, which led to the natural symmetry and harmony of Arda becoming scarred and torn.

✳

Of the Maiar, there were a multitude, but only a few
of these immortals are named in Tolkien's chronicles.

KUMA
(VOID)

ILLUMBAR (Walls of the World)

VAIYA (ETHER)

WEST LAND

AMAN

UTUMNO

ILLUIN (North Lamp)

MIDDLE-EARTH

EAST LAND

EAST SEA

WEST SEA

GREAT LAKE

ISLE OF ALMAREN

ORMAL (South Lamp)

EKKAIA (THE ENCIRCLING SEA)

VISTA (SPHERE OF AIR)

Years 5,000–10,000

THE AGES
OF THE LAMPS

The 'Quenta Silmarillion' and the later publication of Tolkien's drafts and chronologies in 'The Ambarkanta' and the 'Annals of Valinor' tell us of an idyllic time after the time of Creation and the Shaping of Arda. In the Ages of the Lamps, the Valar filled the world with natural wonders of great beauty and harmony, despite the Marring of Arda during the First War. These Ages were so named because the Valar fashioned two colossal lamps with which to light the world.

It was the Vala called Aulë the Smith who forged these golden vessels, while the Star Queen, Varda, and the Wind King, Manwë, filled them and made them radiant with light. It took the combined powers of the other Valar to raise each up on a mighty pillar, taller by far than any mountain. One lamp was placed in the north of Middle-earth and was called Illuin. It stood in the midst of an encircling inland sea called Helcar. The other was in the south and was called Ormal. It stood in the midst of the inland sea called Ringol.

During the Ages of the Lamps, the First Kingdom of the Valar, on the Isle of Almaren, was built in the Great Lake in the midmost point of Arda. Filled with the beautiful mansions and towers of the Valar and Maiar, it was a wonder to see, and the world was filled with joy and light.

This was an idyllic time that was also called the 'Spring of Arda'. Yavanna the Fruitful brought forth the great forests and the wide meadows, and many gentle and beautiful beasts and creatures of field and stream.

OLVAR:
FLORA OF ARDA

Telperion and Laurelin

Galathilion

Celeborn

Nimloth

VALINOR

NÚMENOR

MIDDLE-EARTH

Many of the most beautiful of the flowers of Middle-earth were brought as gifts to mortals from the shores of the Undying Lands by the High Elves of Eldamar

When Númenor was newly made, the Elves of Tol Eressëa brought many fragrant evergreen trees

Brethil
There were once wide forests of birch trees. In the Sindarin language of the Grey-elves, the trees of these lands were called 'Brethil'

Hírilorn

Vardarianna
Vardarianna was a tree 'beloved of Varda'

Oiolairë
Númenórean sea kings blessed their ships with safe passage by cutting a bough of the sacred, fragrant tree called Oiolairë and setting it on the ship's prow

Lairelossë
Lairelossë, meaning 'summer-snow-white', was a fragrant flowering evergreen tree

Taniquelassë
The flower, the leaf and the bark were much prized by the Númenóreans for their sweet scent. Its name suggests that the tree had its origins on the slopes of Taniquetil, the Sacred Mountain of Manwë and the highest mountain in the Undying Lands

Neldoreth
Among the most loved of the trees growing in Middle-earth were those that Elves called Neldoreth but which Men knew as Beech. Taur-na-Neldor, the Forest of Neldoreth, was thought to be the fairest forest in Beleriand

Seregon
On Amon Rûdh, nothing would grow except the hardy Seregon plant. In Elvish its name means 'blood-stone', for when the plant blossomed with its dark red flower the stone summit appeared to be covered in blood

Nan-tasarion
'valley of the Tasarion'

Nimbrethil
Nimbrethil were fair white birch trees

Niphredil
The white flower Niphredil appeared in the forest of Neldoreth at the time of Lúthien's birth

Nessamelda
One of the many fragrant evergreen trees

Yavannamirë
Among the scented evergreen trees was the Yavannamirë, named in honour of Yavanna, the Valarian Queen of the Earth. The name means 'Jewel of Yavanna' and it produced a luscious, round and scarlet fruit

Mariners of Númenor brought Galenas
to Middle-earth

Lissuin
Lissuin was a sweet-
smelling flower

Mallos
In the fields of Lebennin, near
the delta of the River Anduin,
there grew the flowers named
Mallos, the 'gold-snow'

Region
Among the trees
of Middle-earth
was one that Elves
called Region, and
Men called Holly

Galenas
The broad-leafed herb was
prized for the fragrance
of its flowers. It grew
in abundance about
the settlements of the
Númenóreans' descendants.
The Hobbits discovered
Galenas in their own land
and dried and shredded the
leaves. Then they put fire
to them in long-stemmed
pipes. It was afterwards
known on Middle-earth as
Pipe-weed

❀ Simbelmynë ❀
Near Edoras lay the great barrow
graves of the kings. On these graves,
like glittering snow, grew the white
flowers called Simbelmynë, which in the
common speech of Men is 'Evermind'
and by the Elves was known as Uilos

Alfirin
A sad song sung by the
Grey-elves of Middle-
earth tells of a plant
called Alfirin. Its flowers
were like golden bells
and it grew on the green
plain of Lebennin near
the delta lands of the
Anduin

Culumalda
On the river-island of Cair Andros
grew the fairest of the trees of Ithilien.
They were called Culumalda, which
was 'golden red', for such was the hue
of their foliage

Caras Galadhon
'city of trees'

Second, third and
fourth White Trees

Lothlórien

White Tree
of Gondor

Mallorn
Lothlórien was a forest land where
the tallest and loveliest trees of
Middle-earth grew. These were the
Mallorn trees, which had barks of
silver and blossoms of gold, and
from autumn to spring the leaves
were also golden-hued

Brambles of Mordor
The Brambles were
hideous with foot-long
thorns, as barbed and sharp
as the daggers of Orcs, which
sprawled over the land like
coils of steel wire. They were
truly the flowers of the land
of Mordor

❀ Elanor
Elanor, which means
'star-sun', was a fair
winter flower. Its
bloom was star-
shaped and golden

From the land of the Númenóreans, a herb of magical healing powers came to Middle-earth

Tasarion
The Tasarion are the trees Men
now call the Willow

Athelas
In the High Elven tongue this
herb was named Asëa Aranion,
the 'leaf of kings', because
of the special powers that it
possessed in the hands of the
kings of Númenor. Elven-
lore used the Sindarin name,
Athelas; in the common tongue
of Men it was Kingsfoil

Huorns
Mostly, the Huorns stood like
dark trees in the deepest forests,
gnarled and unmoving. When
aroused in wrath they moved
swiftly as if wrapped in shadows

Gallows-weed
In the swamplands of Middle-
earth there grew the Gallows-
weed. In the lore of Hobbits this
tree-hanging weed is known by
name but its properties were not
spoken of

KELVAR: FAUNA OF ARDA

MIDDLE-EARTH

Hummerhorns
Winged insects

Neekerbreekers
In the foul Midgewater
Marshes there lived
creatures akin to crickets

Undead phantoms

Mewlips
An evil race of cannibal spirits

Ancalagon the Black
Uruloki – 'rushing jaws'

Uruloki
Fire-drakes

ANGBAND

Glaurung
Uruloki – Father of Dragons

Barrow-wights
The Undead, who
animated the bones of the
ancient Kings of Men

Carcharoth
'The Red Maw' was
the greatest Wolf of
all time

Balrogs
Huge and hulking,
the Balrogs were
Man-like demons
with streaming manes
of fire and nostrils
that breathed flame

Cold-drakes

Huan

MISTY MOUNTAINS

BELERIAND

Orcs

Eagles

Kirinki
A small bird covered
in brilliant scarlet
plumage and gifted
with a beautiful
piping voice

Eagles

GONDOLIN

Wolves

MORIA

**Dead Men
of Dunharrow**

Balrog

Gothmog the Balrog
Lord of Balrogs

Orcs

Eagles

**'Watcher in
the Water'**

ISENGARD

Orcs

Swans

MENELTARMA

Thuringwethil
Vampire who took on the
form of a huge Vampire Bat
with iron claws

Orcs

Nazgûl

Crébain

Nightingales

**WHITE
MOUNTAINS**

Mearas
White 'horse
princes' of Rohan

**Wilwarin
(Butterflies)**

NÚMENOR

**TOL-IN-
GAURHOTH**

Seabirds

Shadowfax
Greatest of the
Mearas

**Boar of
Everholt**

Ungoliant
The Great Spider

Draugluin
Father
of Werewolves

Huan
Wolfhound of
the Valar

Horses

Orcs

Boar

TANIQUETIL

Werewolves

Uruk-hai

VALINOR

Mûmakil – Oliphaunts
Massive, bad-tempered
beasts, half-way between a
pre-historic mammoth and
an elephant

Eagles of Manwë

Thorondor
Lord of Eagles

Wolves

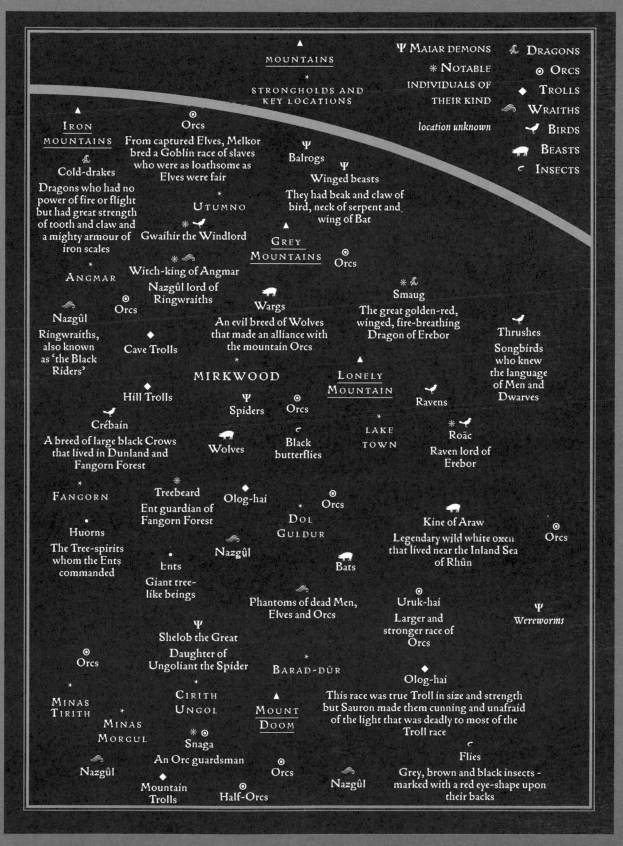

▲ MOUNTAINS

✱ STRONGHOLDS AND KEY LOCATIONS

Ψ MAIAR DEMONS
✱ NOTABLE INDIVIDUALS OF THEIR KIND

location unknown

⚔ DRAGONS
⊙ ORCS
◆ TROLLS
〰 WRAITHS
🐦 BIRDS
🐖 BEASTS
c INSECTS

IRON MOUNTAINS

⊙ Orcs
From captured Elves, Melkor bred a Goblin race of slaves who were as loathsome as Elves were fair

⚔ Cold-drakes
Dragons who had no power of fire or flight but had great strength of tooth and claw and a mighty armour of iron scales

UTUMNO

Ψ Balrogs

Ψ Winged beasts
They had beak and claw of bird, neck of serpent and wing of Bat

🐦 Gwaihir the Windlord

GREY MOUNTAINS

⊙ Orcs

ANGMAR

Witch-king of Angmar
Nazgûl lord of Ringwraiths

⊙ Orcs

Nazgûl
Ringwraiths, also known as 'the Black Riders'

◆ Cave Trolls

🐖 Wargs
An evil breed of Wolves that made an alliance with the mountain Orcs

⚔ Smaug
The great golden-red, winged, fire-breathing Dragon of Erebor

🐦 Thrushes
Songbirds who knew the language of Men and Dwarves

◆ Hill Trolls

MIRKWOOD

Ψ Spiders

⊙ Orcs

LONELY MOUNTAIN

🐦 Ravens

Crébain
A breed of large black Crows that lived in Dunland and Fangorn Forest

🐖 Wolves

c Black butterflies

LAKE TOWN

🐦 Roäc
Raven lord of Erebor

FANGORN

Treebeard
Ent guardian of Fangorn Forest

◆ Olog-hai

⊙ Orcs

DOL GULDUR

🐖 Kine of Araw
Legendary wild white oxen that lived near the Inland Sea of Rhûn

⊙ Orcs

• Huorns
The Tree-spirits whom the Ents commanded

Nazgûl

🐖 Bats

• Ents
Giant tree-like beings

Phantoms of dead Men, Elves and Orcs

⊙ Uruk-hai
Larger and stronger race of Orcs

Ψ Wereworms

Ψ Shelob the Great
Daughter of Ungoliant the Spider

BARAD-DÛR

◆ Olog-hai
This race was true Troll in size and strength but Sauron made them cunning and unafraid of the light that was deadly to most of the Troll race

⊙ Orcs

MINAS TIRITH

CIRITH UNGOL

MOUNT DOOM

MINAS MORGUL

🐦 Snaga
An Orc guardsman

Nazgûl

⊙ Mountain Trolls

⊙ Half-Orcs

Nazgûl

c Flies
Grey, brown and black insects - marked with a red eye-shape upon their backs

THE GREAT LAMPS

In the 'Quenta Silmarillion' we are told that after the First War, the Valar built an idyllic kingdom called Almaren in the Great Lake in the midst of Middle-earth. In the north and the south of Middle-earth they raised two titanic Lamps of Light. However, in the far north, the cruel Vala Melkor raised the Iron Mountains and built his dark kingdom of Utumno. In the ensuing war the Lamps were destroyed, and – in the cataclysm that followed – the Valar fled to the furthest western land of Aman.

✳

The Great Lamps.

THE DESTRUCTION OF THE LAMPS

But Almaren was not the only kingdom built in this time. Far to the north, the rebel Maiar spirits once again gathered, and Melkor again entered Arda. In secret, while the Valar rested from their labours, Melkor raised the vast Iron Mountains like a mighty wall across the northlands and built beneath them a dark fortress called Utumno. From that refuge he began to corrupt the work of the Valar, and poisons seeped into the waters and forests. Yavanna's beautiful creatures were twisted and tortured until they became monstrous and filled with a desire for blood.

At last when he thought he had grown strong enough, Melkor came forth openly with his wicked host and made war on the Valar. Catching them unprepared, he cast down the mighty pillars of the Great Lamps so the mountains were broken, and the consuming flame of the Lamps spread all over the world. In the tumult, the kingdom of Almaren was totally destroyed.

In this terrible conflict, the Spring of Arda was ended, and the world was once again plunged into darkness, except for the destructive fires of the earth, and the tumult of earthquakes and rushing seas. It required all the strength of the Valar hosts to quell these mighty upheavals, lest the world itself be entirely destroyed. Rather than do battle with Melkor in the midst of such tumult and cause further destruction, the Valar abandoned Almaren and Middle-earth altogether. They went into the furthermost west, to the great continent of Aman, which later was called the Undying Lands. So the Ages of the Lamps ended with the Valar making a new kingdom in the West, while all the wrecked lands of Middle-earth were left in thrall to the evil power of Melkor.

✳

Following page: The great lamps wrought destruction upon the land as they fell.

THE
UNDYING
LANDS

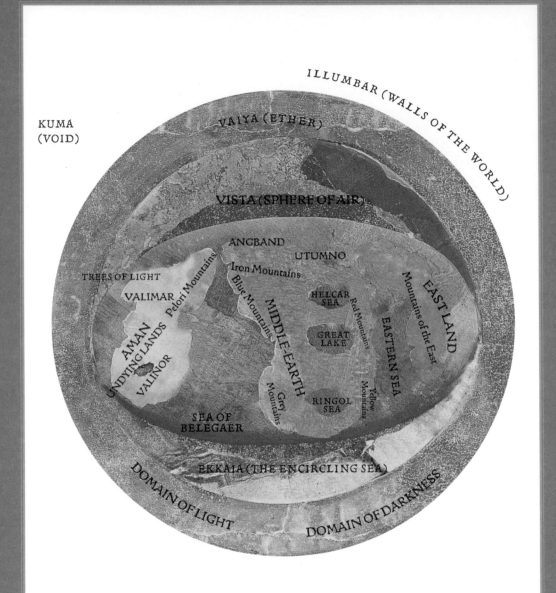

KUMA
(VOID)

ILLUMBAR (WALLS OF THE WORLD)

VAIYA (ETHER)

VISTA (SPHERE OF AIR)

ANGBAND

UTUMNO

Iron Mountains

TREES OF LIGHT

Pelori Mountains

EAST LAND

Mountains of the East

VALIMAR

Blue Mountains

HELCAR SEA

MIDDLE-EARTH

Red Mountains

AMAN
UNDYING LANDS
VALINOR

GREAT LAKE

EASTERN SEA

Yellow Mountains

Grey Mountains

RINGOL SEA

SEA OF
BELEGAER

EKKAIA (THE ENCIRCLING SEA)

DOMAIN OF LIGHT

DOMAIN OF DARKNESS

Years 10,000–20,000

THE AGES OF THE TREES

The Valar built a new kingdom called Valinor on the continent of Aman in the west. Beyond the gates of their city of Valimar they grew the Trees of Light.

These mighty trees filled all the Undying Lands of Aman with a blessed light. Meanwhile, Middle-earth and the rest of Arda was plunged into the Ages of Darkness. Melkor ruled as master of Middle-earth from his heinous realm of Utumno. He also built his second stronghold of Angband, and placed it under the command of his loyal disciple, Sauron.

Following page: The trees filled Valinor
with radiant light.

THE TREES
OF LIGHT

After the destruction of the Great Lamps and the First Kingdom of Almaren, the Valar went west to the continent of Aman, where they built a second kingdom called Valinor, meaning 'Land of the Valar'. There they each took a part of that land and raised mansions and created gardens, but also built Valimar, the 'Home of the Valar', a walled city with domes and spires of gold and silver that was filled with the music of many bells.

On a hill just outside the western golden gates of Valimar, the Valar grew two huge, magical trees. These were the tallest trees that ever grew and were called Laurelin the Golden and Telperion the White. Nearly the size of the Lamps of the Valar, these Trees of Valinor gave off a brilliant glow of gold and silver light. The waxing and waning of each Tree's blossoming gave a means by which the days might be measured, and their light nourished all who lived within the glowing presence.

We learn from Tolkien's early drafts of the chronicles, in the 'Annals of Valinor', that the Ages of the Trees began one thousand Valarian Years after the creation of Arda; that is, the Tenth Valarian Age, or ten thousand mortal years after the Creation. We also learn that the Ages of the Trees were nearly twenty Valarian Ages, or twenty thousand mortal years, in duration.

There is, however, a complicating factor in Tolkien's chronology of Arda because the Ages of the Trees apply only to the Undying Lands. We are told that upon arriving in Aman, the Valar raised up a great wall in the form of the Pélori Mountains to keep out Morgoth and all his minions. These mountains, the tallest in the world, did indeed protect Valinor from invasion, but they also shut in the Light of the Trees.

Consequently during the Ages of the Trees we are dealing with parallel systems of time. So, while the Undying Lands were basking in the glory of the Trees, Middle-earth underwent two epochs, each lasting ten thousand mortal years: the Ages of Darkness and the Ages of the Stars.

Nimloth: the White Tree of Númenor, descended
from Telperion the Silver Tree of the Valar.

THE PEACE OF ARDA

In the Undying Lands, the Ages of the Trees were divided into two eras. The first ten Valarian Ages, or ten thousand mortal years, of the Ages of the Trees were known as the Years of Bliss in Valinor. During this time the Valar and Maiar prospered. The Eagles were created by Manwë, the Ents were conceived by Yavanna, and the Dwarves were conceived by Aulë. Blissful indeed were the times in Valinor, while beyond the walls of the Pélori Mountains, Middle-earth endured the terror and evil of Melkor's dominion during the Ages of Darkness.

During the next ten Valarian Ages, we learn much more of events in Valinor and Middle-earth. This second era of the Ages of the Trees was called the Noontide of the Blessed, but upon Middle-earth it was called the Ages of the Stars. This was the time when Varda, the Queen of the Heavens, rekindled the stars above Middle-earth and caused the Awakening of the Elves.

In time, when news reached the Undying Lands of Melkor's attempts to slay and corrupt the Elves, the Valar made a council of war. The Valar and the Maiar came into Middle-earth and drove Melkor's legions wailing before them.

This was called the War of Powers and in that war were many battles and duels wherein the Valar utterly destroyed Utumno. Thereafter, Melkor was held captive in Valinor and bound with unbreakable chains. This time was known as the Peace of Arda, and lasted through most of the remaining Ages of the Trees in Valinor and Ages of Stars on Middle-earth.

THE SUMMONING OF THE ELVES

These were the great years for the Elven race, for without the hateful wrath of Melkor, these chosen people prospered and grew ever more powerful. After the War of Powers, the Valar summoned the Elves to come and live with them in the Land of Light. This was the mass migration called the Great Journey of the Eldar, those Elves who answered the call of the Valar.

The Great Journey was the theme of many an Elven song, for the time was long, and the Eldar were divided into diverse races. Those who reached the Undying Lands were of three kindreds: the Vanyar, the Noldor and the Teleri. For those chosen people, the Valar gave a part of the Undying Lands called Eldamar, the 'Elven-home', and it was a wonder to behold. Many were its mansions, but the finest were in the Vanyar and Noldor capital of Tirion, and the Teleri cities of Alqualondë on the coast and Avallónë on the Isle of Tol Eressëa.

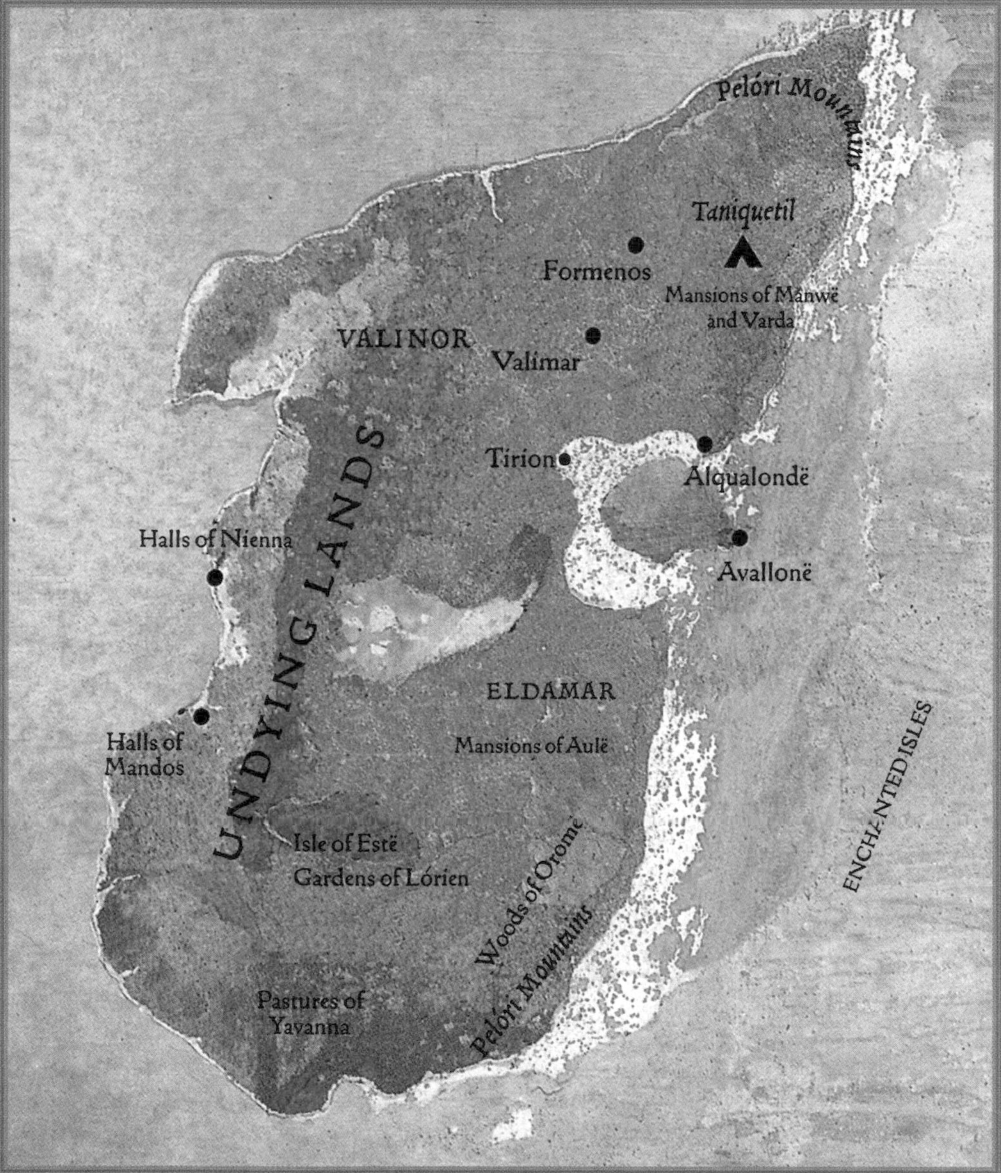

Pelóri Mountains

Taniquetil

Formenos

Mansions of Manwë
and Varda

VALINOR

Valimar

Tirion

Alqualondë

Halls of Nienna

Avallonë

UNDYING LANDS

ELDAMAR

Mansions of Aulë

Halls of
Mandos

Isle of Estë
Gardens of Lórien

Woods of Oromë

ENCHANTED ISLES

Pelóri Mountains

Pastures of
Yavanna

AMAN

THE

UNDYING

LANDS

V A L I N O R

E K K A I A

LAURELIN

TELPERION

Valmar

Ezellohar   Ring
of
Doom

Nienna

Estë

Lorellin

Halls of
Mandos

Woods of Oromë

Mansions
of Aulë

Gardens of Lórien

Pastures of Yavanna

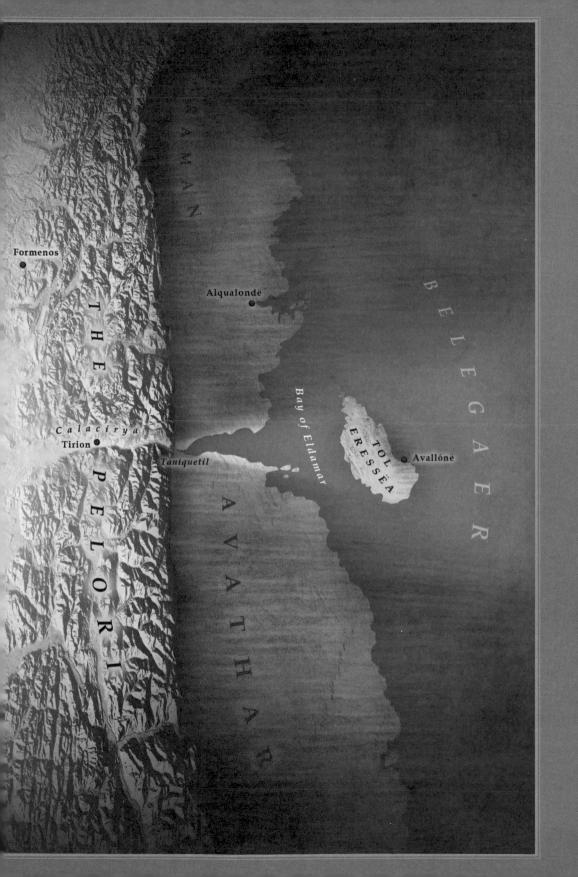

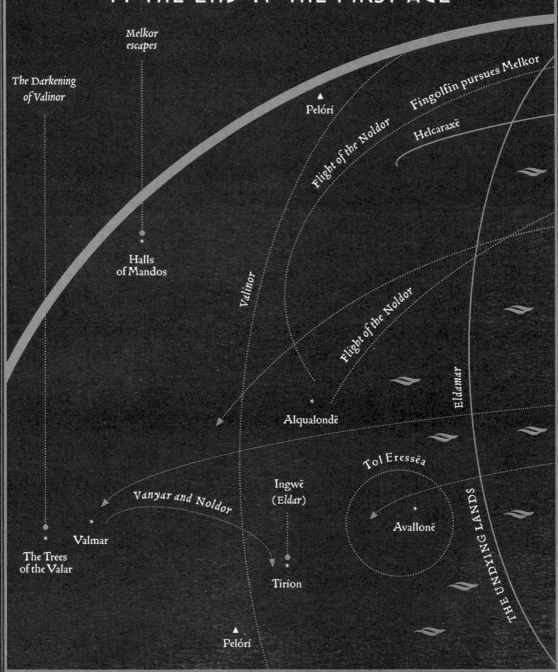

THE JOURNEYS OF THE ELVES FROM THEIR AWAKENING TO THE END OF THE FIRST AGE

Melkor escapes

The Darkening of Valinor

Pelóri

Fingolfin pursues Melkor

Flight of the Noldor

Helcaraxë

Halls of Mandos

Valinor

Flight of the Noldor

Eldamar

Alqualondë

Tol Eressëa

Ingwë (Eldar)

Vanyar and Noldor

Avallonë

THE UNDYING LANDS

Valmar

The Trees of the Valar

Tirion

Pelóri

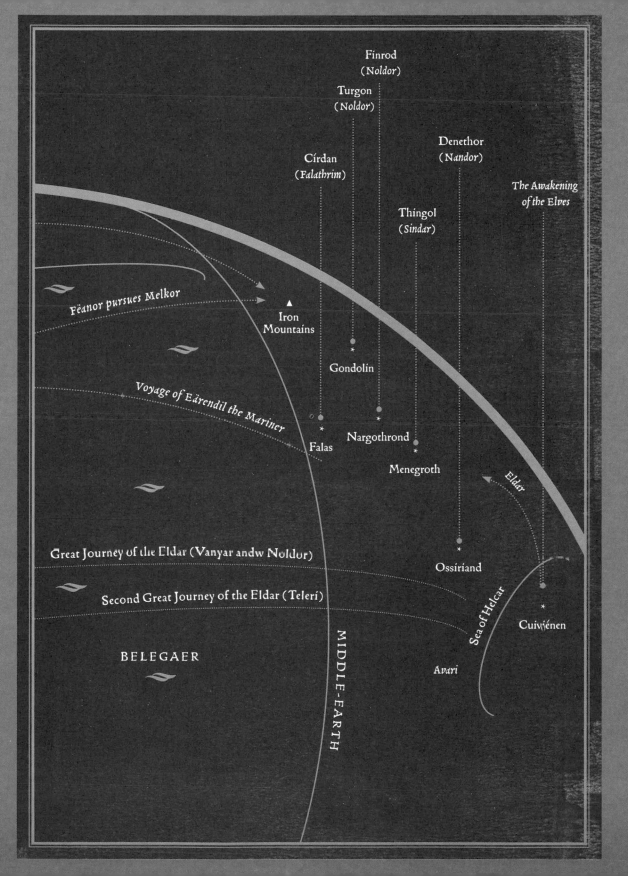

Finrod
(*Noldor*)

Turgon
(*Noldor*)

Denethor
(*Nandor*)

Círdan
(*Falathrim*)

The Awakening
of the Elves

Thingol
(*Sindar*)

▲ Iron
Mountains

Féanor pursues Melkor

Gondolin

Voyage of Eärendil the Mariner

Nargothrond

Falas

Menegroth

Eldar

Great Journey of the Eldar (Vanyar andw Noldor)

Ossiriand

Second Great Journey of the Eldar (Teleri)

Sea of Helcar

Cuiviénen

BELEGAER

MIDDLE-EARTH

Avari

The Haven of Alqualondë was home to the
white ships of the Teleri.

THE HAVEN OF ALQUALONDË

On the shores of the Undying Lands the Teleri built Alqualondë, which is 'haven of swans', and the ships of these Elves were like swans with eyes and beaks of jet and gold. Beneath the arch of sea-carved stone that is the gate of Alqualondë, the Teleri set sail their swan ships, sing fair songs, and listen to the murmuring sea on the shore.

THE CITY OF TIRION

In the Undying Lands, the Noldor and Vanyar Elves built the first and greatest city in Eldamar. This was Tirion of the white towers and crystal stair, and it was set on the hill of Túna in Calacirya, the Pass of Light. The city was placed so that not only could the Elves live in the Light of the Trees and look out on the sea, but also, from under the shadow of Túna and the tall towers, could view the glittering stars that are so dear to their hearts.

Following page: The fair city of Tirion was
home to the Noldor and the Vanyar.

Melkor and Ungoliant looked with hatred
upon the light of the Valar.

THE DARKENING OF VALINOR

After the Ages of Chaining, Melkor came before the Valar to be judged. He seemed to have changed, and claimed to have repented, so Manwë, the Lord of the Valar, ordered his chains to be removed. But the Valar were deceived for Melkor only *seemed* to be fair and good; in secret he plotted their downfall. First he sowed strife among the Elves, and then in alliance with the Great Spider Ungoliant he made open war on the Valar. He came with Ungoliant to the Trees of the Valar and struck them with a great spear, and the Spider sucked the light and life from the Trees so they withered and died. All of Valinor was made hideously black with the Unlight of Ungoliant, and Melkor laughed with villainous joy because, for a second time, he had put out the great Lights of the World.

THE FLIGHT
OF THE NOLDOR

After the destruction of the Trees of the Valar, Melkor slew Finwë, the Noldor king, and took the Silmarils from him. In great wrath the Noldor pursued the evil Vala, and, despite the warning by the Valar, they made their way back to Middle-earth. Some went in ships, which they took from the Teleri, but a great number, led by Fingolfin, crossed Helcaraxë, the Grinding Ice. This was the northern narrow gap of sea and ice between the Undying Lands and Middle-earth. In that crossing many an Elf lord and lady fell into the sea or perished beneath collapsing towers of ice.

The bitter hardships of crossing the
Helcaraxë claimed many Noldor lives.

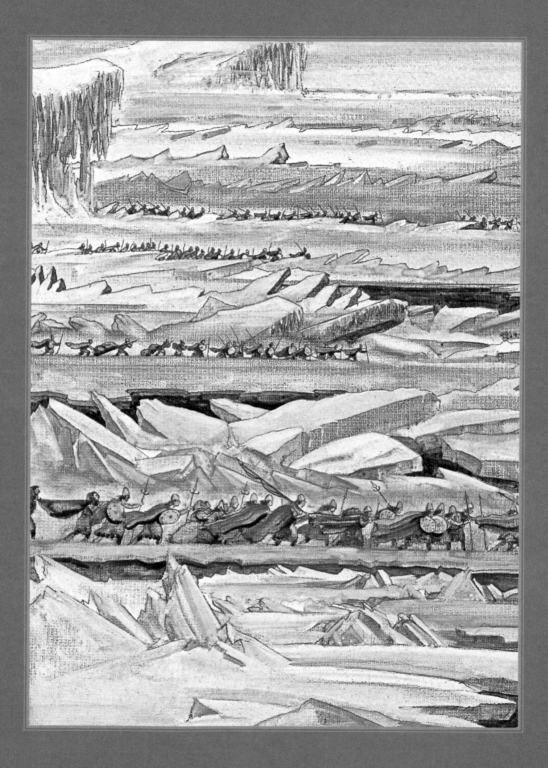

MIDDLE-
EARTH

Melkor's hordes bred in the
darkness of Utumno.

THE AGES OF DARKNESS

While Valinor and the Undying Lands were bathed in the Light of the Trees, all the lands of Middle-earth were plunged into gloom. These were the Ages of Darkness on Middle-earth, when Melkor dug the Pits of Utumno ever deeper beneath the Iron Mountains. With evil splendour, he fashioned hellish, subterranean palaces with vast domed halls, labyrinthine tunnels, and fathomless dungeons out of black stone, fire, and ice.

Here the Lord of Darkness gathered all the bad powers of the world. Their numbers seemed without limit, and Melkor never tired of creating new and ever more dreadful forms. Cruel spirits, phantoms, wraiths and vile demons stalked the halls of Utumno. All the serpents of the world were bred in the pits of a dark kingdom that was home to werewolves and vampires and innumerable bloodfeeding monsters, and insects that flew, crawled and slithered. Within Utumno, all were commanded by Melkor's demon disciples, the fiery Maiar spirits called the Balrogs, with their whips of flame and their black maces. Greatest among these was the High Captain of Utumno, Gothmog the Balrog.

Nor was Utumno Melkor's only kingdom. At the beginning of the Ages of Darkness, Melkor rejoiced in his victory over the Valar, and his destruction of Almaren and the Great Lamps of Light. Thereafter, he strove to increase his power, and in the westernmost part of the Iron Mountains he built a second kingdom. This was the great armoury and stronghold called Angband, the 'Iron-Prison'.

Then he proclaimed the mightiest disciple, Sauron the Maia Sorcerer, the Master of Angband. Except for the watchful eye of Manwë the windlord, looking down from the sacred mountain of Taniquetil, and the occasional visitations of Oromë, the Wild Horseman, among all the Valar only Yavanna, the protector of forests and meadows, entered Middle-earth in those days. Upon all the flora and fauna that she created, she cast a protecting spell called the Sleep of Yavanna, so they might survive the darkness and wickedness of Melkor's rule.

And so, for the most part, these were the Ages of Glory for Melkor, the Lord of Darkness. By his destruction of the Lamps of Light, Melkor inherited the whole of the wrecked and darkened lands of Middle-earth. There he held dominion for ten thousand mortal years.

MORGOTH

Melkor was one of the greatest of the spirits who dwelt with Eru the One before the creation of Arda. Yet he introduced discord to the Music of the Ainur, and when he entered Arda he worked against the other Valar, creating ruin and chaos. He expended so much of his spirit doing evil and dominating his armies that, unlike the other Valar, he had to take permanent fleshly form. When the Eldar came to Middle-earth and strove against him, they named him Morgoth, the Black Foe of the World.

**The Vala Melkor became Morgoth,
Lord of Darkness.**

The Balrogs were the most feared
servants of Melkor.

BALROGS
OF UTUMNO

The Balrog 'demons of might' were the most terrible of the
Maiar spirits to become the servants of Melkor, the Dark
Enemy. Huge and hulking, Balrogs were massive man-like
demons with streaming manes of fire and nostrils that breathed
flame. They seemed to move with clouds of black shadows and
their limbs had the coiling power of serpents. The chief weapon
of the Balrogs was the many-thonged whip of fire, although they
were also known to use the mace, the axe and the flaming sword.
In each of Melkor's battles, Balrogs were his foremost champions,
and so, when the holocaust of the War of Wrath ended Melkor's
reign forever, it largely ended the Balrogs as a race. It was said that
some fled that last battle and buried themselves deep in the roots
of mountains, but after thousands of years nothing more was heard
of these demons. However, during the Third Age of the Sun, the
deep-delving Dwarves of Moria released by accident an entombed
demon. Once unleashed, the Balrog struck down two Dwarf kings;
then, gathering legions of Orcs and Trolls to his aid, drove the
Dwarves from Moria forever. His dominion remained uncontested
for two centuries, until his duel with Gandalf the Grey on the
Bridge of Khazad-dûm.

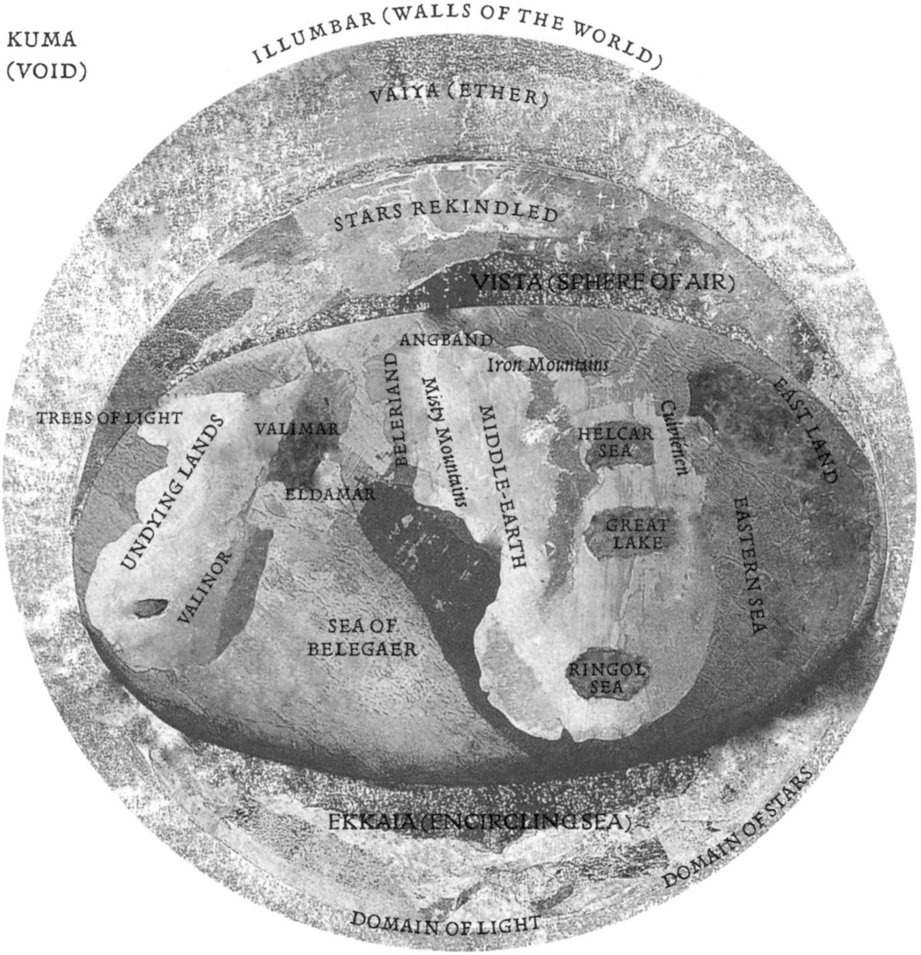

KUMA
(VOID)

ILLUMBAR (WALLS OF THE WORLD)

VAIYA (ETHER)

STARS REKINDLED

VISTA (SPHERE OF AIR)

ANGBAND
Iron Mountains

TREES OF LIGHT

BELERIAND

Misty Mountains

VALIMAR

MIDDLE-EARTH

HELCAR
SEA

Culvérien

EAST LAND

UNDYING LANDS

ELDAMAR

GREAT
LAKE

EASTERN SEA

VALINOR

SEA OF
BELEGAER

RINGOL
SEA

EKKAIA (ENCIRCLING SEA)

DOMAIN OF STARS

DOMAIN OF LIGHT

Years 20,000–30,000

THE AGES OF STARS

When the Undying Lands entered its second era of the Trees of Light, Middle-earth began its Ages of the Stars. This resulted in the Awakening of the Elves, and eventually the War of Powers, when the Valar destroyed Utumno and took Melkor captive. The Elves began their westward migration and founded kingdoms both in Middle-earth and Eldamar in the Undying Lands. Then the seemingly repentant Melkor revolted once more, destroyed the Trees of Light and stole the Silmaril jewels.

THE REKINDLING
OF THE STARS

After many Ages of Darkness, Varda, the Lady of the Heavens, took the dew from the Silver Tree of the Valar, and, crossing the skies, rekindled the faint stars which shone down on Middle-earth, so they became brilliant and dazzling in the velvet night. The creatures of Melkor were so unused to light that they screamed in pain when these shafts of starlight pierced their dark souls. In terror, they fled and hid themselves away.

Yet, above all, the Rekindling of the Stars signified the Awakening of the Elves. For when the stars shone down on Middle-earth, the Elves awoke with starlight in their eyes, and something of that light remained there forever after. The place of awakening was the Mere of Cuiviénen by the shores of Helcar, the inland sea beneath the Orocarni, the Red Mountains.

The Ages of the Stars was also the time of the awakening of the two other speaking peoples: the Dwarves, who were conceived by Aulë the Smith, and the Ents, who were conceived by Aulë's spouse, Yavanna the Fruitful. Then, too, in the pits of Utumno, Melkor bred two other races. These were the Orcs and the Trolls, twisted life forms made from tortured Elves and Ents who fell into his hands.

When Oromë the Horseman discovered the Awakening of the Elves, and the Valar learned of the wickedness done to them by Melkor, they held a council of war. The Valar and Maiar came to Middle-earth arrayed for battle against Melkor.

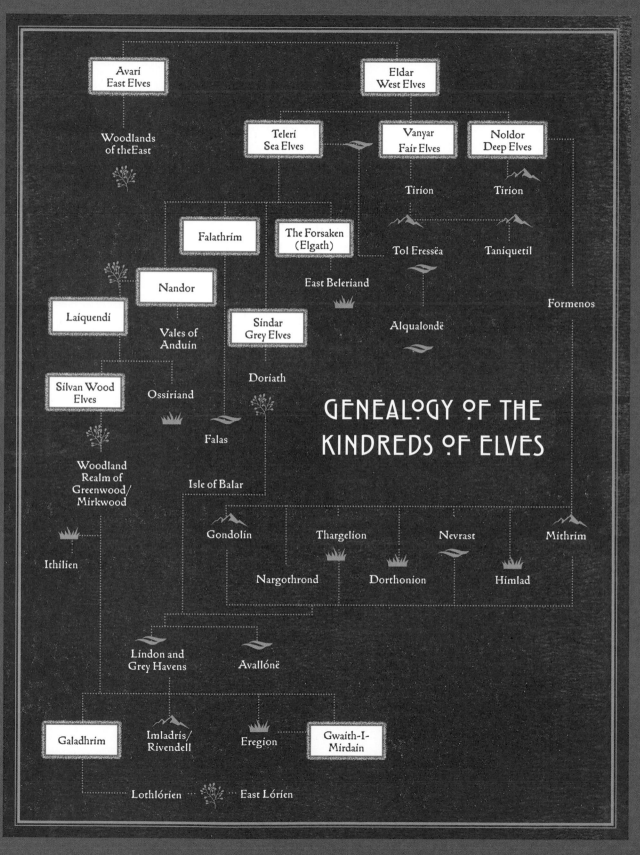

GENEALOGY OF THE KINDREDS OF ELVES

Avari
East Elves

Eldar
West Elves

Teleri
Sea Elves

Vanyar
Fair Elves

Noldor
Deep Elves

Woodlands
of the East

Tirion

Tirion

Falathrim

The Forsaken
(Elgath)

Tol Eressëa

Taniquetil

Nandor

East Beleriand

Formenos

Laiquendi

Síndar
Grey Elves

Alqualondë

Vales of
Anduin

Silvan Wood
Elves

Ossiriand

Doriath

Falas

Woodland
Realm of
Greenwood/
Mirkwood

Isle of Balar

Gondolin

Thargelion

Nevrast

Mithrim

Ithilien

Nargothrond

Dorthonion

Himlad

Lindon and
Grey Havens

Avallónë

Galadhrim

Imladris/
Rivendell

Eregion

Gwaith-I-
Mírdain

Lothlórien

East Lórien

The Awakening of the Elves.

THE GREAT JOURNEY

During this War of Wrath they slew Melkor's evil legions, broke down the great wall of the Iron Mountains, and utterly destroyed Utumno. Melkor's dominion over Middle-earth was ended. He was bound with chains and held prisoner in Valinor for many ages. This was the period known as the Peace of Arda, and was the time of the Great Journey, when the Elves made their mass westward migration to Eldamar, on the shores of the Undying Lands. For the most part these were glorious years for the Elves in both Middle-earth and the Undying Lands.

The High Elves who succeeded in completing the Great Journey and who settled in Eldamar, built the wonderful cities of Tirion, Alqualondë and Avallónë. Yet many others, for love of the lands of Middle-earth, remained behind. They built their kingdom in mortal lands and lived glorious lives.

During the Ages of Stars there was a great kingdom of Elves in Beleriand in the northwest of Middle-earth. These were the Elves of the Teleri kindred who followed King Thingol and Queen Melian the Maia. They were called the Grey Elves, or the Sindar, and their kingdom was the vast forestland of Doriath. Their greatest city was called Menegroth of the Thousand Caves, and the caverns and grottoes of their citadel were one of the wonders of Middle-earth. The lords of the Sindar were the masters of Beleriand and the mightiest Elves upon Middle-earth in the Ages of Stars. Their allies were the Sea Elves of the Falas, the Laiquendi (or Green Elves) of Ossiriand, and the Dwarves of Belegost and Nogrod in the Blue Mountains. The Ages of Stars lasted ten thousand mortal years, and were ages of discovery and wonder, of glory and magic. Yet, all this was ended when Melkor was at last released from captivity in Valinor. After a time of seeming penance, he rose up in wrath and destroyed the Trees of the Valar. Then he fled into the north of Middle-earth, where he once again inhabited his fortress of Angband in the Iron Mountains. The Peace of Arda ended as the conflict spread to Beleriand, and the Ages of Stars came to an end.

THE AWAKENING OF THE DWARVES

In a great hall under the mountains of Middle-earth, Aulë, the Smith of the Valar, fashioned the Seven Fathers of the Dwarves during the Ages of Darkness.

Ilúvatar was aware of Aulë's presumptuous deed, and would not permit that this race should come forth before his chosen children. Yet he judged that Aulë acted without malice. Therefore he sanctified the Dwarves, and bade Aulë set them to sleep for many ages.

In the years that followed the Awakening of the Elves, the seven Fathers of the Dwarves stirred, and their stone chamber was broken open. They arose and were filled with awe. Each of the Seven Fathers made a great mansion under the mountains of Middle-earth, but the Elven histories of these early years speak only of three. Those were Belegost and Nogrod in the Blue Mountains, and Khazad-dûm in the Misty Mountains.

Dwarves of the Mountains.

The Dwarves explored the wondrous caves
beneath the mountains.

THE AWAKENING
OF THE ENTS

After the Rekindling of the Stars and the Awakening of the Elves, the Ents also awoke in the great forests of Arda. They came forth from the thoughts of Yavanna, Queen of the Earth. Also known as the Shepherds of Trees, the Ents were giant guardians of the forests. They were half men, half trees in appearance, with skin like rough bark and branchlike arms with seven-fingered hands. They were fourteen feet tall and could stand unmoving for years at a time, or could move swiftly on unbending legs taking giant 'Ent strides' with feet like living roots. The eldest Ents were believed to have inhabited Middle-earth for over nine ages of stars and sun. Although most often patient and wise beings, if roused to anger they could crush stone and steel with their bare hands. During the War of the Ring, the wrath of the Ents was unleashed against Saruman the Wizard of Isengard.

✳

The Shepherds of the trees.

The dread race of Orcs was bred from Elves
who were corrupted by Melkor.

THE BREEDING OF THE ORCS

Within the deepest pits of Utumno, in the First Age of Stars, it is said that Melkor – whom the Elves gave the name Morgoth, meaning the 'Dark Enemy' – committed his greatest blasphemy. For in that time he captured many of the newly risen race of Elves and took them to his dungeons, and with vile acts of torture he made ruined and terrible forms of life. From these he bred a goblin race of slaves who were as loathsome as Elves were fair. These were the Orcs, a multitude brought forth in shapes twisted by pain and hate. Their stunted form was hideous: bent, bow-legged and squat. Their arms were as long and strong as apes. The jagged fangs in their wide mouths were yellow, their tongues red and thick, and their nostrils and faces were broad and flat. Their eyes were crimson gashes, and glowed like hot red coals. Orcs were fierce warriors, for they feared more greatly their master than any enemy, and perhaps death was preferable to the torment of Orkish life. They were flesh-eating cannibals, dwellers of foul pits and tunnels, who hunted by night, and were fearful of light. More quickly than any other beings of Arda their progeny came forth from the spawning pits of the Dark Enemy to fill the ranks of his armies.

Melkor's greatest blasphemy.

BELERIAND KINGDOMS IN THE FIRST AGE

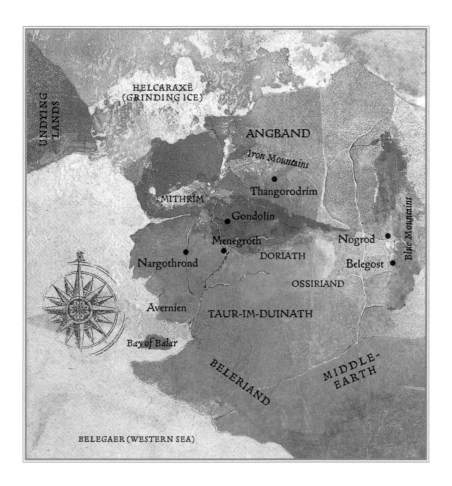

BELERIAND

During the Ages of the Stars, Beleriand became the homeland of the Sindar Grey Elves. Their capital was Menegroth in the forests of Doriath. In the First Age of the Sun, the Noldor Elves returned and founded Nargothrond, Gondolin and many other kingdoms. However, all of these were destroyed, along with Menegroth and Melkor's Angband, in the Wars of Beleriand. At the end of the Age, Beleriand sank beneath the waves.

✳

The Lost Lands of Ladros.

THE THOUSAND CAVES OF MENEGROTH

Through the Ages of Stars, while the High Elves of Eldamar flourished in the Light of the Trees, on Middle-earth the Sindar Grey-elves became a great race. Their king was Elu Thingol and their queen was Melian the Maia. The Sindar were lords of all Beleriand and they lived in the citadel of Menegroth, the Thousand Caves. This place was a wonder to all the World because the Sindar loved the forests so greatly. The halls and caverns of Menegroth were carved with trees, birds and animals of stone and filled with fountains and lamps of crystal, and through these halls walked the Sindar lords, the greatest Elves of Middle-earth in the Ages of Stars.

THE RISING OF THE SUN

Although the Trees of the Valar had been destroyed, the Valar Yavanna and Nienna coaxed from their scorched ruins a single flower of silver called Isil the Sheen and a single fruit of gold called Anor the Fire-golden. This flower and this fruit were placed in great vessels that became the Moon and the Sun, which were carried across the skies by Maiar spirits. It is said that with the rising of the Sun there came the Awakening of Men in the eastern land of Hildórien on Middle-earth. So began the Ages of the Sun in which the race of mortal Men flourished and spread over all the lands of Middle-earth.

Previous page: The halls of Menegroth
were filled with wonders.

The race of Men awakened at
the rising of the Sun.

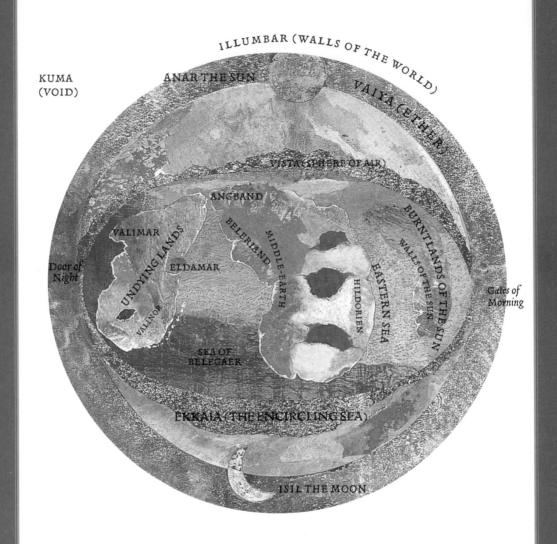

KUMA
(VOID)

ILLUMBAR (WALLS OF THE WORLD)

ANAR THE SUN

VAIYA (ETHER)

VISTA (SPHERE OF AIR)

ANGBAND

VALIMAR

UNDYING LANDS

ELDAMAR

BELERIAND

MIDDLE-EARTH

BURNTLANDS OF THE SUN

WALLS OF THE SUN

Door of
Night

VALINOR

HILDORIEN

EASTERN SEA

Gates of
Morning

SEA OF
BELEGAER

EKKAIA (THE ENCIRCLING SEA)

ISIL THE MOON

Years 30,000–30,601

THE FIRST AGE OF THE SUN

The Valar created the Sun and the Moon. This resulted in the Awakening of Men in Hildórien in the east. The Noldor Elves entered Beleriand in pursuit of Melkor, and laid siege to Angband for the first four centuries of the War of the Jewels. However, in 455 the siege was broken, and Angband's legions destroyed the Elven kingdoms one by one. Finally, the Valar returned and in the War of Wrath, destroyed Angband and cast Melkor out forever into the Void.

The glowing vessels were carried
up into the heavens.

THE FIRST DAWN

Although the Ages of the Sun are the main focus for virtually all Tolkien's tales, the Sun does not arise in the sky until the Thirtieth Valarian Age, or some 30,000 mortal years after the creation of Arda. And yet, even the time span in Sun years is monumental. By the end of the War of the Ring and the Third Age, no less than 7,063 mortal years had passed.

In the early chronologies of 'The Annals of Valinor', Tolkien tells us that 29,980 mortal years after the creation of Arda, Melkor and the Great Spider Ungoliant ended the Ages of the Trees in Valinor and put out the Trees' light forever. Yet the Valar Yavanna and Nienna saved a single flower of silver from Telperion and a single fruit of gold from Laurelin. These were placed in great vessels forged by Aulë the Smith, and in the 30,000th mortal year since the creation of the world, these glowing vessels were carried up into the heavens. These vessels were the Moon and the Sun, and ever afterwards they lighted all the wide lands of Arda.

THE AWAKENING OF MEN

As the Rekindling of the Stars marked the Awakening of the Elves, so the Rising of the Sun signalled the Awakening of Men. When the first light of dawn entered the eyes of Men, they awoke to a new age. For, as Ilúvatar had conceived the race of Elves at the beginning of Time and hid them away in the Meres of Cuiviénen, so he also conceived of the mortal race of Men and hid them in the east of Middle-earth in a place called Hildórien, the 'land of the followers' beyond the Mountains of the Wind.

In strength of body and spirit, these new people compared poorly with the Elves. They were mortals and were short-lived even compared to the Dwarves. Out of pity, the Elves taught this sickly people what they could, only to find that in their mortality was a secret strength. For this race proved more adaptable to the demands of a changing world, and although they died easily, and in great numbers, they bred more quickly than any race save the Orcs.

Tribes of these wandering peoples travelled over the lands of Middle-earth. The best and the strongest among them were the Edain, those who first entered the Eldar kingdoms of Beleriand.

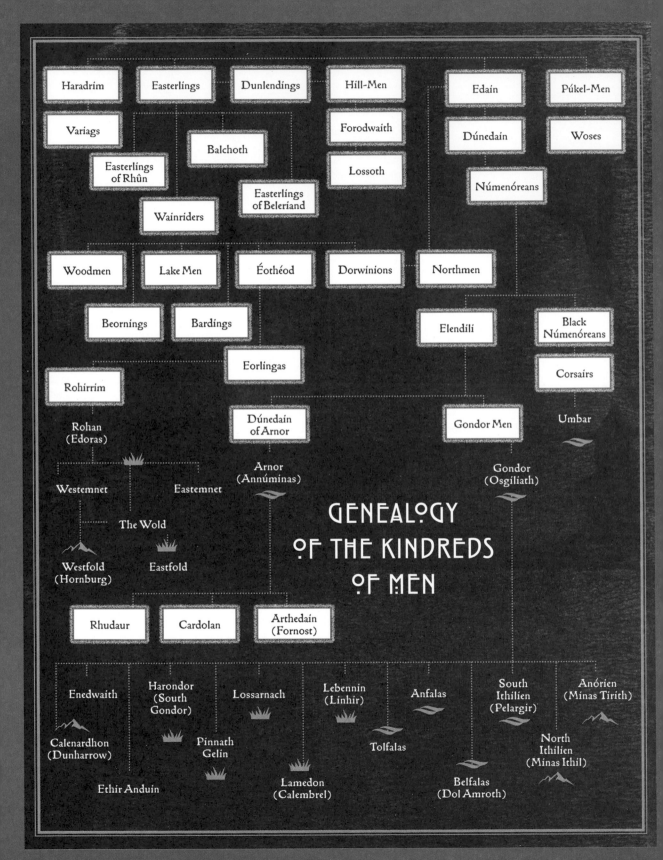

GENEALOGY OF THE KINDREDS OF MEN

Haradrim

Easterlings

Dunlendings

Hill-Men

Edain

Púkel-Men

Variags

Balchoth

Forodwaith

Dúnedain

Woses

Easterlings of Rhûn

Lossoth

Númenóreans

Easterlings of Beleriand

Wainriders

Woodmen

Lake Men

Éothéod

Dorwinions

Northmen

Beornings

Bardings

Elendili

Black Númenóreans

Eorlingas

Corsairs

Rohirrim

Dúnedain of Arnor

Gondor Men

Umbar

Rohan (Edoras)

Westemnet

Eastemnet

Arnor (Annúminas)

Gondor (Osgiliath)

The Wold

Westfold (Hornburg)

Eastfold

Rhudaur

Cardolan

Arthedain (Fornost)

Enedwaith

Harondor (South Gondor)

Lossarnach

Lebennin (Linhir)

Anfalas

South Ithilien (Pelargir)

Anórien (Minas Tirith)

Calenardhon (Dunharrow)

Pinnath Gelin

Tolfalas

North Ithilien (Minas Ithil)

Ethir Anduin

Lamedon (Calembel)

Belfalas (Dol Amroth)

THE SILMARILS

The First Age of the Sun was the Heroic Age that began with the coming of Noldor High Elves out of Eldamar in pursuit of Melkor, whom they called Morgoth, the Dark Enemy. For not only had Morgoth destroyed the Trees of Light, but he also stormed the Elven fortress of Formenos, slew the High King of the Noldor, and seized the magical jewels called the Silmarils. These three gems were the greatest treasure of the Noldor, for they had been fashioned by them from the light of the Trees of the Valar. It was the struggle for possession of these gems that resulted in the War of the Great Jewels, and gave Tolkien his theme for *The Silmarillion*. It was a conflict lasting six centuries and distinguished by six major battles.

Morgoth extinguished the Trees of Light, seized the Silmarils and fled to Angband some twenty mortal years before the dawning of the First Age of the Sun. The Wars of Beleriand began a decade later, when he sent his Orkish leaders against the Elves of Beleriand. This was the First Battle in which the Orkish hordes were eventually routed and driven back into Angband. The Second Battle was fought four mortal years before the rising of the Sun and was called the Battle Under Stars, Dagor-os Giliath. The forces of Morgoth came against the newly arrived Noldor Elves in north-western Beleriand. Although outnumbered, the Noldor fought ferociously for ten days. They slaughtered all before them and forced the Orcs to retreat to Angband.

WARS OF BELERIAND

Darkening of Valinor

Theft of Silmarils

First Battle of Beleriand

Battle-Under-Stars (Dagor-os-Giliath)

1 Battle of Lammoth

6º The Glorious Battle (Dagor Aglareb)

16º Orc raids on Hithlum

26º Dragon attack out of Angband

455 Battle of Sudden Flame (Dagor Bragollach)

457 Fall of Tol Sirion

468 Quest of the Silmaril

473 Battle of Unnumbered Tears (Ninaeth Arnodiad)

496 Battle of Tumhalad, Sack of Nargothrond

5º6 Sack of Menegroth

511 Fall of Gondolin

Journeys of Eärendil the Mariner

C.6º1 The Great Battle, Angband Destroyed

AGES OF STARS

AGES OF STARS

Wars of the Jewels

FIRST AGE OF THE SUN

The Long Peace

Siege of Angband

War of Wrath

THE WARS OF BELERIAND

In the year 56 of the First Age of the Sun, the forces of Morgoth had regained sufficient strength to send out an army greater than the two previous armies combined. This Third Battle was called the Glorious Battle, Dagor Aglareb, for not only did the Elves overthrow Morgoth's Orc legions, they cut off their retreat and annihilated them. So complete was the victory that for nearly four centuries the Elves kept a close guard on Angband. During this time there were Orc raids on Hithlum, and in 260 Glaurung the Dragon attempted an attack, but for the most part there was peace in Beleriand. Few of Morgoth's servants dared to venture south of the Iron Mountains. However, when Morgoth finally broke the Long Peace, he was truly prepared. In the year 455, his legions of Orcs were led by Balrogs and fire-breathing dragons. This was the Fourth Battle which was called the Battle of Sudden Flame, or Dagor Bragollach. This was followed by the Fifth Battle, the Battle of Unnumbered Tears, or Ninaeth Arnodiad. These two battles resulted in total victory for Morgoth and the eventual destruction of all the Elven kingdoms of Beleriand. In 496, Nargothrond was sacked. Shortly thereafter Menegroth was ruined, and 511 marked the fall of Gondolin, the last of the Elven strongholds.

For nearly a century Morgoth maintained his iron grip over Middle-earth. Finally the Valar and Maiar could no longer tolerate his wickedness, and in the year 601 they came forth a third and final time to make war on the Dark Enemy in the cataclysm called the War of Wrath and the Great Battle. So terrible was this conflict that not only was Angband destroyed, but so too were all the fair lands of Beleriand. And though Morgoth called up all his monsters and demons, and even a legion of fire-breathing dragons, he was overthrown and cast out forever to the Void. Yet, this victory had its price. Beleriand was ruined. The Iron and Blue Mountains were broken apart, and the great waters were let in. All Beleriand was flooded, and eventually sank beneath the Western Sea. So ended the First Age of the Sun.

Following page: The Battle of Sudden Flame.

THE BATTLE OF SUDDEN FLAME

For nearly four centuries the Elves kept a close watch on Angband, and Beleriand enjoyed peace. But Morgoth was not idle, and in the year 455 smoke and fire belched forth from Thangorodrim, and under the cover of darkness and clouds of ash a vast force of Balrogs, Orcs and fire-breathing dragons erupted from Angband. Elves and the Edain fought valiantly side by side, but they were beaten back, relentlessly. Within sixty years, all of the Elven kingdoms of Middle-earth were either destroyed or occupied by hostile forces.

THE QUEST OF THE SILMARIL

While armies of thousands perished in the long War of the Jewels and the Battle of Sudden Flame, it was only by the efforts of two star-crossed lovers – the mortal Beren and the Elf princess Lúthien – that one of the three stolen Silmarils was won back from the terrible Valarian lord, Morgoth, the Dark Enemy. This was achieved in the Quest of the Silmaril when by the power of the spells of Lúthien, the lovers gained entry into the great armoury and underground fortress of Angband. There in the horror of its nethermost chamber, Lúthien – the most beautiful child of the Elven race – stood before the throne of Morgoth the Dark Enemy, and sang a wondrous song of enchantment.

Lúthien before Morgoth.

GOTHMOG
THE BALROG

Gothmog, Lord of Balrogs, was one of the greatest and most terrible of the spirits who came to Arda with Melkor. He bore a whip of flame, and sometimes wielded a great black axe. During the wars of Beleriand, he led armies of Balrogs, Orcs and Trolls, and laid waste to many lands of Elves, Dwarves and Men. His greatest challenge came when he faced Ecthelion of Gondolin, during the terrible sack of the Hidden City.

*

Glorfindel battles a Balrog.

The hidden city of Gondolin fell to the might of Morgoth, the Dark Enemy.

THE FALL OF GONDOLIN

The most beautiful Elven city built on Middle-earth was said to be Gondolin, the Hidden Kingdom. This was the last Elf-Kingdom to survive the War of the Jewels. Its king was Turgon, the Noldor lord, who wisely chose to conceal the city in the Encircling Mountains. But in the end the Servants of Morgoth discovered it, and Orc legions appeared before its gates, together with Trolls and fire-breathing dragons driven on by the Balrog demons. Though the Elves battled valiantly Gondolin was sacked, and with its destruction the Elf-realms of Beleriand were brought to an end.

THE DESTRUCTION OF ANGBAND

After watching the defeats and sufferings of the Elves and Men of Beleriand, the Valar could no longer tolerate the evil dominion of Morgoth over the lands of Middle-earth. So the Valar and Maiar joined in the War of Wrath against Morgoth's cruel kingdom of Angband. All the world was rent by this great war. The Iron Mountains were broken open, and the dungeons and great chambers of torture were destroyed. Morgoth's dragons and demons came into battle but were slain by the Valarian host. The servants of Morgoth were scattered, and he himself was cast into the Void. So ended the First Age of the Sun, and with it the chief architect of wickedness vanished forever, though much that Morgoth had made remained within the Spheres of the World.

Tuor and Voronwë seek Gondolin.

Angband could not withstand
the wrath of the Valar.

NÚMENÓREAN EMPIRE IN THE SECOND AGE

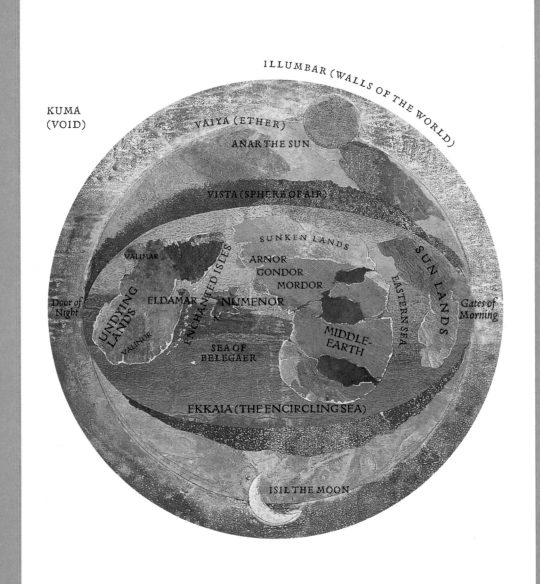

KUMA
(VOID)

ILLUMBAR (WALLS OF THE WORLD)

VAIYA (ETHER)

ANAR THE SUN

VISTA (SPHERE OF AIR)

SUNKEN LANDS

VALIMAR

ARNOR
GONDOR
MORDOR

SUN LANDS

Door of
Night

UNDYING
LANDS

ELDAMAR

ENCHANTED ISLES

NÚMENOR

EASTERN SEA

Gates of
Morning

VALINOR

MIDDLE-
EARTH

SEA OF
BELEGAER

EKKAIA (THE ENCIRCLING SEA)

ISIL THE MOON

Years 30,601–34,042

THE SECOND AGE
OF THE SUN

The second age was the Age of the Númenóreans. As has been told in the 'Akallabêth' or 'The Downfall of Númenor', these were Men who were descended from the Edain of the First Age and to whom the Valar had given the newly created land in the midst of the wide sea between Middle-earth and the Undying Lands.

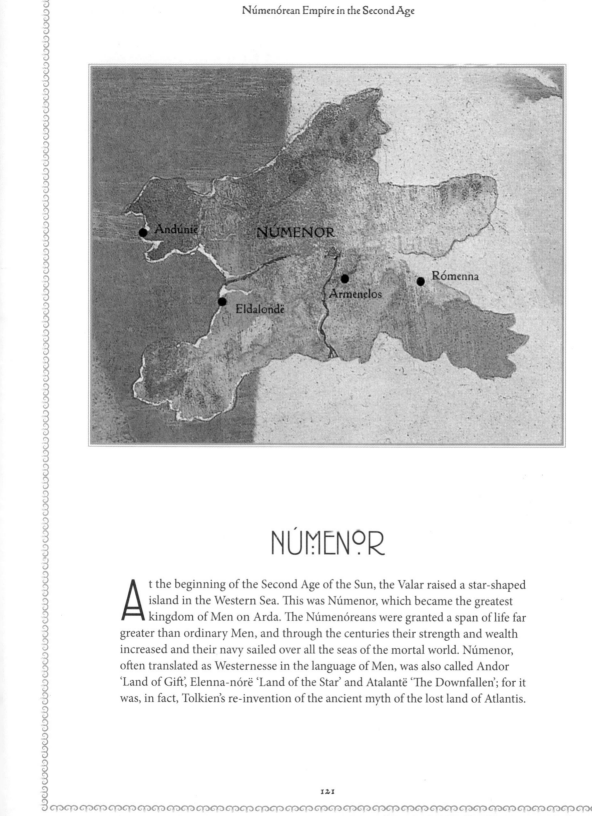

NÚMENOR

At the beginning of the Second Age of the Sun, the Valar raised a star-shaped island in the Western Sea. This was Númenor, which became the greatest kingdom of Men on Arda. The Númenóreans were granted a span of life far greater than ordinary Men, and through the centuries their strength and wealth increased and their navy sailed over all the seas of the mortal world. Númenor, often translated as Westernesse in the language of Men, was also called Andor 'Land of Gift', Elenna-nórë 'Land of the Star' and Atalantë 'The Downfallen'; for it was, in fact, Tolkien's re-invention of the ancient myth of the lost land of Atlantis.

A CHRONOLOGY OF THE SECOND AGE

1 Foundation of Lindon, under Gil-galad

32 Foundation of Númenor, with Elros as its first king

c. 500 Sauron reappears in Middle-earth

c. 750 Establishment of Eregion (Hollin) by Celebrimbor

c. 775 Foundation of Vinyalondë, the first Númenórean haven in Middle-earth

1000 Sauron begins to build Barad-dûr, the Dark Tower, in Mordor

c. 1350 Galadriel and Celeborn settle in Lothlórien

1590 Celebrimbor forges the Three Rings

1600 Sauron forges the One Ring – the Year of Dread

1693 The War of the Elves and Sauron begins

1697 Fall of Eregion and the foundation of Imladris (Rivendell)

1700 Númenóreans defeat Sauron at the Battle of Gwathló

1701 First White Council is held

2709 Ar-Adûnakhôr is the first Númenórean king to take an Adûnaic royal name

3117 Númenóreans ban the use of the Elven tongue

3177 Civil war breaks out in Númenor between the King's Men and the Faithful

3255 Ar-Pharazôn seizes the Sceptre

3262 Ar-Pharazôn takes Sauron prisoner

3319 Downfall of Númenor and the Changing of the World;
Sauron flees back to Middle-earth

3320 Foundation of the Realms in Exile, Arnor and Gondor

3430 Last Alliance formed between the Númenóreans in exile and the Elves

3431 Last Alliance marches to Imladris

3434 Battle of Dagorlad followed by the Siege of Barad-dûr

3441 Deaths of Gil-galad and Elendil; defeat of Sauron; Isildur takes the One Ring

LAND OF THE STAR –
NAMES AND PENTACLES

In *The Return of the King* (1955), the third volume of *The Lord of the Rings*, readers discovered extensive appendices that included the Annals of the Kings. Here, Tolkien explained how the Edain – the noble and heroic Men who survived the wars of the First Age – sailed westward over the Great Sea and 'guided by the Star of Eärendil' came at last to 'the great Isle of Elenna, western most of all Mortal lands'. And it was on that great island continent that the Edain settled and founded the kingdom of Númenor.

However, it was not until the posthumous publication of *The Silmarillion* (1977) – some forty years after Númenor's original conception – that readers learned the name Elenna could be translated from Elvish to mean 'starwards', or 'Land of the Star'. This revelation left readers with the impression that the island was so called because of the guiding light of the 'Star of Eärendil'. And yet, this was far from being the full story.

Readers would have to wait another four years for the publication of the second posthumous book, *Unfinished Tales of Númenor and Middle-earth* (1980), to learn the most obvious explanation for the name Elenna 'Land of the Star' was, in fact, geographic. In *Unfinished Tales*, it is explained for the first time: 'The land of Númenor resembled in outline a five pointed star, or pentacle'.

This account – also for the first time – is accompanied by a map of the star-shaped island along with an extensive description of the geographic, horticultural, political and social organization of Númenor.

⁕

'Star of Eärendil'.

THE ISLAND OF NÚMENOR

The map published in *Unfinished Tales* was created by Christopher Tolkien many years after his father's death. That map was based upon the father's written texts and an unpublished 'little rapid sketch, the only one, as it appears, that my father ever made of Númenor'. Consequently, the published map, although not entirely authoritative, provides an adequate model for Númenor's overall geography along with the location of its major cities, harbours and provinces.

Tolkien's Númenor was an island kingdom shaped like a five-pointed star. At its narrowest, it measured two hundred and fifty miles across, and nearly twice that distance from the farthest promontories. It was divided into six regions: one for each peninsula and one for its heartland, where stood the sacred mountains, Meneltarma, or 'pillar of heaven', the tallest mountains on Númenor. On its slopes stood Armenelos, the 'city of kings', where the king and the largest single number of Númenóreans lived. Farther below was the royal port of Rómenna. The other prominent city-ports, Eldalondë and Andúnië, faced west towards the Undying Lands.

*

'Pillar of Heaven'.

ELVEN AND
HALF-ELVEN RULERS

The first king of Númenor was Elros, son of Eärendil and the twin brother of Elrond Half-elven. At the end of the First Age, when the Half-elven twins were told by the Valar that they must choose their fate, Elrond chose that of the immortal Elves, while Elros became king of the mortal Edain. However, being Half-elven, he was granted a life-span of five hundred years and he ruled as the king of Númenor until the year 442 of the Second Age. While the Númenóreans prospered on their island, the High Elves of Middle-earth gathered under the banner of Gil-galad, the last High Elf-king in the realm of Lindon. The Sindar Grey Elves established kingdoms among the Silvan Elves in Greenwood the Great and the Golden Wood of Lothlórien in the Vales of the Great River, Anduin. In the eighth century, the Noldor Elves of Celebrimbor established the kingdom of the Elven-smiths of Eregion, just to the west of the Dwarf kingdom of Khazad-dûm in the Misty Mountains. However, another power also prospered in this time, for Sauron the Sorcerer remained in the mortal world and secretly conspired to succeed Melkor as the Dark Lord of Middle-earth.

✳

Following page:
The Sack of Eregion.

KINGS AND QUEENS
OF NÚMENOR

1. Elros Tar-Minyatur
r. F.A. 532–S.A. 422
D. 32–422

2. Tar-Vardamir
r. 61–471
D. 422

3. Tar-Amandil
r. 192–603
D. 422–590

4. Tar-Elendil
r. 350–751
D. 590–740

5. Tar-Meneldur
r. 543–942
D. 740–883

6. Tar-Aldarion
r. 700–1098
D. 883–1075

7. Tar-Ancalimë
r. 873–1285
D. 1075–1280

8. Tar-Anárion
r. 1003–1404
D. 1280–1394

9. Tar-Súrion
r. 1174–1574
D. 1394–1556

10. Tar-Telperiën
r. 1320–1731
D. 1556–1731

11. Tar-Minastir
r. 1474–1873
D. 1731–1869

12. Tar-Ciryatan
r. 1634–2035
D. 1869–2029

13. Tar-Atanamir
r. 1800–2221
D. 2029–2221

14. Tar-Ancalimon
r. 1986–2386
D. 2221–2386

Tar-Anducal (Herucalmo)
r. 2286–2657
D. 2637–2657
*Considered a usurper and
therefore not counted as one
of the kings*

15. Tar-Telemmaitë
r. 2136–2526
D. 2386–2526

16. Tar-Vanimeldë
r. 2277–2637
D. 2526–2637

17. Tar-Alcarin
r. 2406–2737
D. 2637–2737

18. Tar-Calmacil
r. 2516–2825
D. 2737–2825

19. Tar-Adramin
r. 2618–2899
D. 2825–2899

20. Ar-Adûnakhôr
r. 2709–2962
D. 2899–2962

21. Ar-Zimrathôn
r. 2798–3033
D. 2962–3022

22. Ar-Sakalthôr
r. 2876–3102
D. 3033–3102

23. Ar-Gimilzôr
r. 2960–3177
D. 3102–3177

24. Tar-Palantir
r. 3035–3255
D. 3177–3255

25. Ar-Pharazôn
r. 3318–3319
D. 3255–3319

ANNÚMINAS
founded
3320
by Elendil

ELOSTIRION
founded after
3320
by Elendil

AMON SÛL
founded after
3320
by Elendil

Arnor

ORTHANC
likely founded
between
3320 and 3340
by the
Dúnedain

Gondor

Mordor

MINAS
ANOR
founded
3320
by
the Faithful

OSGILIATH
founded
c. 3319
by
Isildur and
Anarion

MINAS
ITHIL
founded
c. 3320
by
the Faithful

BARAD-
DÛR
founded
1000
by Sauron

KINGDOMS & FORTRESSES
OF THE SECOND AGE

THE RISE
OF SAURON

In the year 1000, Sauron secretly began to build his odious realm of Mordor, enslaving the barbarian races of Men of the East and South and gathering Orcs and other beings to his kingdom. He also began building the Dark Tower of Barad-dûr. He assumed the fair form of one named Annatar, meaning 'lord of gifts' in Quenya, and attempted to seduce the Elves with his wisdom and power. Only Celebrimbor and the Elven-smiths of Eregion were deceived. Using the combined powers of magic and metallurgy, Sauron and the Elven-smiths collaborated in the making of many fantastic creations. By the year 1500, they reached the peak of their ability and, under Sauron's instruction, began to forge the Rings of Power. By 1600, all the Rings were completed, and Sauron treacherously returned to Mordor, where he completed the building of the Dark Tower of Barad-dûr and forged the One Ring, thus becoming the Lord of the Rings. When the Elven-smiths realized they had been duped into helping Sauron become the all-powerful Lord of the Rings they rose up against him, and from 1693 to 1701 the bloody War of the Elves and Sauron raged. In that conflict Sauron slew Celebrimbor, destroyed the city of the Elven-smiths, ruined Eregion, and overran nearly all of Eriador. The Dwarves of Khazad-dûm retreated from the conflict and shut their doors on the world. Thereafter, this hidden realm was known as Moria, the 'black chasm' in Sindarin. In the terrible struggle most of the Elves of Eregion were slain; only a small number survived. These were led by Elrond Half-elven into the foothills of the Misty Mountains, where they founded the colony of Imladris, which Men later called Rivendell.

After his victory over Celebrimbor, Sauron gathered his forces and marched against Gil-galad in Lindon. At the last moment, a mighty fleet of Númenóreans joined the Elvish ranks. Sauron's legions were utterly crushed, and he was forced to retreat to Mordor.

SAURON AND THE NÚMENÓREANS

For a thousand years Sauron made no move against the Elves, but worked instead among the barbarian Easterlings and Haradrim tribes. Among their savage kings, he distributed the Nine Rings of Mortal Men. By the twenty-third century they had become the Nazgûl, his chief servants, who Men knew as the Ringwraiths. Meanwhile, the Númenóreans had become the mightiest sea power the world had ever seen. On the coastlands of Middle-earth they created many colonies, as well as the fortress-ports of Umbar and Pelagir.

In the year 3261, the Númenóreans landed a huge armada at Umbar and disgorged a massive force that marched on Mordor. When Sauron saw their terrible might, all the peoples of the world were amazed to see the Ring Lord descend from his Dark Tower and surrender himself unto them.

The Númenóreans put Sauron in chains, took him to their own land and imprisoned him in their strongest dungeon. But, by guile, Sauron achieved that which he could not by strength of arms. He falsely counselled the proud Númenórean kings and corrupted them, so they plotted against the Valar themselves. So successful was this corruption that the Númenóreans dared to raise the greatest fleet of ships that ever was, and sailed into the west to make war on the Powers of Arda. For this act, Ilúvatar caused the fair island of Númenor to burst asunder. The mountains and the cities fell, the sea arose in wrath and all Númenor collapsed into a watery abyss.

❋

The Nazgûl bow before Sauron.

THE CHANGE
OF THE WORLD

In that cataclysm came the Change of the World. The Undying Lands were set beyond the Spheres of the World and were forever beyond the reach of all but the Chosen, who travelled in Elven ships along the Straight Road. This was the end of the Age of Atlantis as we now know it in myths, and the world turned in on itself. It was no longer a flat world bounded by the Encircling Sea and enclosed within the Sphere of Air and Ether, but became the globed planet that we now know it to be.

But the Second Age did not end with the sinking of Númenor in the year 3319, nor did the heritage of its people vanish. For as the tales of the time tell, there were those among the Númenóreans who were led by the Princes of Andúnië, who called themselves the Faithful and refused to forsake the Valar and the Eldar. Led by Elendil the Tall, they sailed nine ships eastward toward the shores of Middle-earth at the moment of the cataclysm. These were the Dúnedain, the faithful surviving Númenóreans, who established the kingdoms of Arnor and Gondor upon Middle-earth.

Yet soon there was strife and conflict, for, by the power of the One Ring, Sauron also escaped the sinking of Númenor and returned to Mordor, wherein he plotted to destroy all remaining Elvish and Dúnedain kingdoms upon Middle-earth.

THE LAST ALLIANCE

In retaliation, the Last Alliance of Elves and Men formed, and Sauron's army was defeated at the Battle of Dagorlad. Entering Mordor itself, the Alliance laid siege to the Dark Tower for seven long years before Sauron was overthrown. In this last struggle, the Dúnedain High King Elendil and his son Anárion, along with the last High King of the Eldar on Middle-earth, Gil-galad, were all slain before the Dúnedain King Isildur at last cut the One Ring from Sauron's hand. With the conquest of Mordor, the destruction of the Dark Tower, the banishment of the Ringwraiths, and the downfall of Sauron, in the year 3441, the Second Age came to an end.

✳

The Dúnedain King Isildur cut the One
Ring from Sauron's hand.

THE BLACK NÚMENÓREANS

The port and city of Umbar was the most powerful outpost of the Númenóreans on Middle-earth during the Second Age. Corrupted by Sauron the Ring Lord, they survived the downfall and the Change of the World. Just as the 'Faithful' Númenóreans who founded the Dúnedain kingdoms of Arnor and Gondor among the North Men of Middle-earth, the Black Númenóreans of Umbar formed a powerful alliance with the Men of the South, known as the Haradrim. Throughout the Third Age, powerful armadas of the black ships frequently sailed out of Umbar to join forces with the allies of Mordor against their sworn enemies, the Dúnedain in the north kingdoms of Arnor and Gondor.

Umbar was a colony of Númenor until its
capture by the Men of the South.

DÚNEDAIN KINGDOMS IN THE THIRD AGE

UNDYING LANDS

EARTH'S ATMOSPHERE

THE STRAIGHT ROAD

ARNOR
RHÛN
GONDOR
MORDOR
MIDDLE-EARTH
HARAD

INLAND SEA

WEST SEA

FAR HARAD

HITHER
LANDS

EAST SEA

SUNLANDS

SOLAR SYSTEM

DARK LANDS

✳

Years 34,042–37,063

THE THIRD AGE
OF THE SUN

The globed, mortal world was forever separated from the Undying Lands. Only the ships of the Elves were permitted to sail the Straight Road to reach it. At the end of the Second Age, the Dúnedain – or surviving Númenóreans – founded Arnor and Gondor, and with the Elves destroyed Sauron and Mordor. However, the Ring Lord secretly returned in the Third Age and rebuilt Mordor. Finally, Sauron's plots against the Dúnedain and the Elves culminated in the War of the Ring.

SAURON CORRUPTED

At first, Sauron was one of the Maiar of Aulë, but he was soon corrupted by Morgoth, and he became the Dark Lord's chief lieutenant. When Morgoth was cast into the Void at the end of the First Age, Sauron returned to Middle-earth, calling himself Annatar, 'giver of gifts', and appearing to offer friendship to the Elves of Eregion and the Men of Númenor. He taught the Elves the art of making Rings of Power, but unknown to them, he forged for himself the One Ring, which controlled all the others. Finally the Númenóreans made war on Sauron, and he fought with their leaders before the gates of Barad-dûr. In the Third Age, he took the form of a great lidless eye, ceaseless in his search for the One Ring, which seemingly had been lost forever.

THE DARK TOWER
OF MORDOR

By the power of the Ruling Ring, Sauron made the foundations of Barad-dûr, the Dark Tower of Mordor. The Last Alliance of Elves and Men laid siege to that Tower for seven years at the end of the Second Age before finally forcing Sauron into open battle. Though many of the greatest Eldar and Dúnedain lords were slain, the Alliance was granted victory and the One Ring was cut from Sauron the Ring Lord's hand.

For more than a thousand years Sauron had no shape and wandered Earth as a powerless shadow. Yet because the One Ring was not destroyed, Sauron and his Tower were not ended. Both he and the tower were to arise in the Third Age, and once again Sauron the Ring Lord would seek to dominate the world.

The dreadful tower of Barad-dûr loomed
over Mordor.

A CHRONOLOGY OF
THE KINGDOMS OF MIDDLE-EARTH

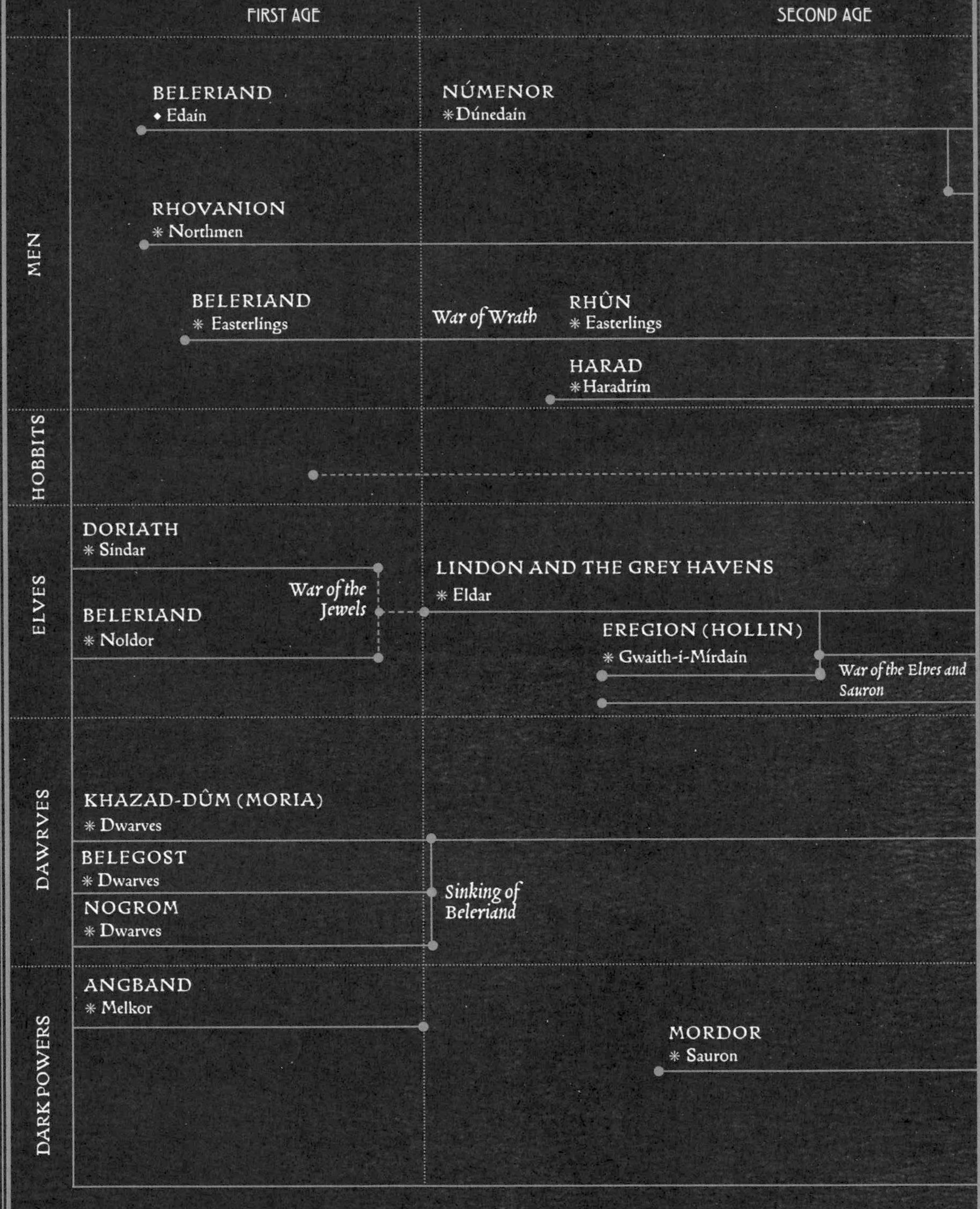

MEN

BELERIAND
◆ Edain

NÚMENOR
＊ Dúnedain

RHOVANION
＊ Northmen

BELERIAND
＊ Easterlings

War of Wrath

RHÛN
＊ Easterlings

HARAD
＊ Haradrim

HOBBITS

ELVES

DORIATH
＊ Sindar

War of the Jewels

LINDON AND THE GREY HAVENS
＊ Eldar

BELERIAND
＊ Noldor

EREGION (HOLLIN)
＊ Gwaith-i-Mírdain

War of the Elves and Sauron

DAWRVES

KHAZAD-DÛM (MORIA)
＊ Dwarves

BELEGOST
＊ Dwarves

Sinking of Beleriand

NOGROM
＊ Dwarves

DARK POWERS

ANGBAND
＊ Melkor

MORDOR
＊ Sauron

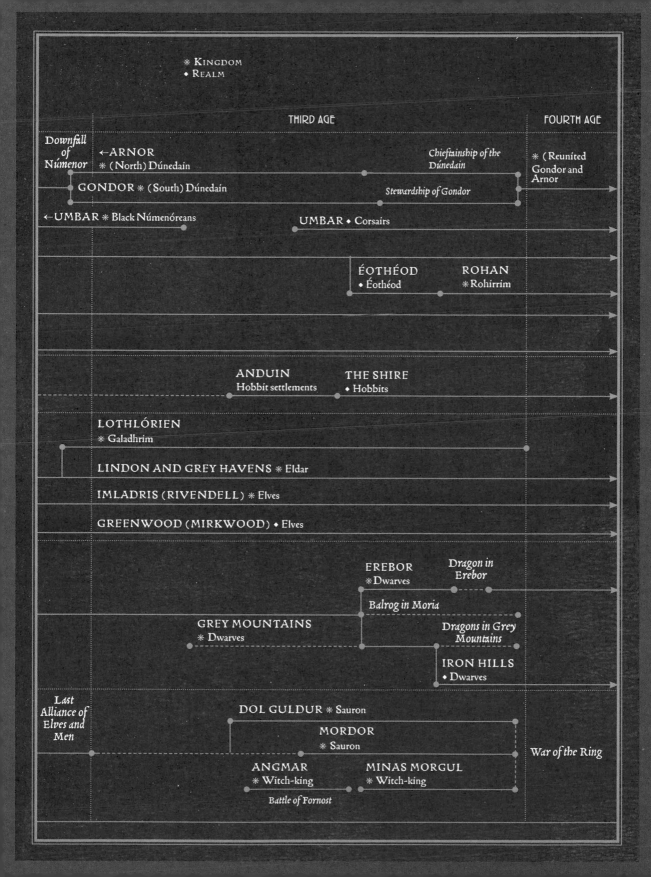

* Kingdom
♦ Realm

THIRD AGE   FOURTH AGE

Downfall of Númenor

←ARNOR
* (North) Dúnedain
                                                    Chieftainship of the Dúnedain

GONDOR * (South) Dúnedain
                                                    Stewardship of Gondor

* (Reunited Gondor and Arnor

←UMBAR * Black Númenóreans   UMBAR ♦ Corsairs

ÉOTHÉOD
♦ Éothéod   ROHAN
                             * Rohirrim

ANDUIN
Hobbit settlements   THE SHIRE
                            ♦ Hobbits

LOTHLÓRIEN
* Galadhrim

LINDON AND GREY HAVENS * Eldar

IMLADRIS (RIVENDELL) * Elves

GREENWOOD (MIRKWOOD) ♦ Elves

EREBOR
* Dwarves   Dragon in Erebor

                            Balrog in Moria

GREY MOUNTAINS
* Dwarves   Dragons in Grey Mountains

                            IRON HILLS
                            ♦ Dwarves

Last Alliance of Elves and Men

DOL GULDUR * Sauron

MORDOR
* Sauron

ANGMAR
* Witch-king   MINAS MORGUL
                            * Witch-king

Battle of Fornost

War of the Ring

GONDOR
AND ARNOR

The two dominant concerns of Tolkien's history of the Third Age of the Sun are the survival of the Kingdoms of Gondor and Arnor, and the not unrelated fate of the One Ring of Sauron, the Ring Lord.

At the end of the Second Age, when Sauron the Ring Lord was overthrown, it was Isildur, the High King of the United Kingdom of Gondor and Arnor, who cut the One Ring from his hand.

At the time, this was deemed a righteous act and the only means of destroying the power of the Dark Lord; however, once Isildur himself seized the One Ring, a part of him was corrupted by its evil power. For strong and virtuous though he was, Isildur could not resist its promise of power.

Though he stood on the volcanic slopes of Mount Doom itself, in whose fires the Ring was forged and the only place where it could be unmade, he could not bring himself to destroy it. Isildur succumbed to temptation and took the One Ring as his own, and thus its curse soon fell upon him. In year two of the Third Age, Isildur and his three eldest sons were marching northward through the Vales of Anduin when the entourage was ambushed by Orcs.

This was the Battle of Gladden Fields which resulted in the death of Isildur and his three sons and the loss of the One Ring in the waters of the River Anduin. The disastrous consequences of Gladden Fields took over 3,000 years to right. The loss of the One Ring meant that the wicked spirit of Sauron could not be brought to rest until the Ring was found and destroyed, while the death of the High King of the United Kingdom of the Dúnedain resulted in the splitting of the realm into two separate kingdoms: Arnor and Gondor.

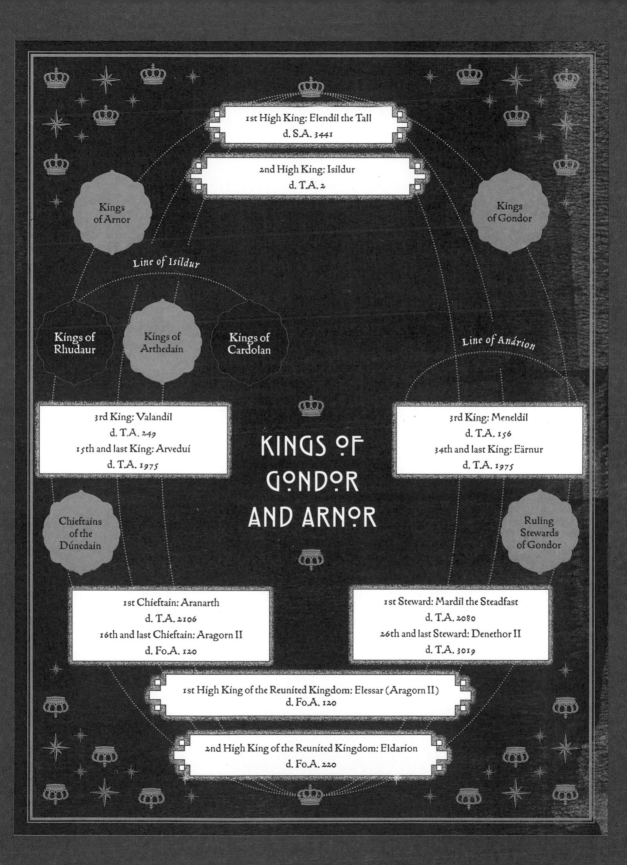

KINGS OF GONDOR AND ARNOR

1st High King: Elendil the Tall
d. S.A. 3441

2nd High King: Isildur
d. T.A. 2

Kings of Arnor

Kings of Gondor

Line of Isildur

Kings of Rhudaur

Kings of Arthedain

Kings of Cardolan

Line of Anárion

3rd King: Valandil
d. T.A. 249
15th and last King: Arvedui
d. T.A. 1975

3rd King: Meneldil
d. T.A. 156
34th and last King: Eärnur
d. T.A. 1975

Chieftains of the Dúnedain

Ruling Stewards of Gondor

1st Chieftain: Aranarth
d. T.A. 2106
16th and last Chieftain: Aragorn II
d. Fo.A. 120

1st Steward: Mardil the Steadfast
d. T.A. 2080
26th and last Steward: Denethor II
d. T.A. 3019

1st High King of the Reunited Kingdom: Elessar (Aragorn II)
d. Fo.A. 120

2nd High King of the Reunited Kingdom: Eldarion
d. Fo.A. 220

THE CURSE
OF THE RING

In effect, because Isildur succumbed to the temptation of the One Ring, the curse of the Ring was visited on the whole of the Dúnedain people. This curse of the Ring consumed the whole of the Third Age, for the United Kingdom could not be healed and made whole again until the One Ring was destroyed and a single legitimate heir (who had the strength to resist the temptations of the Ring) was recognized by the whole of the Dúnedain people. Only then could a High King once again rule in the Reunited Kingdom of the Dúnedain.

Nevertheless, during the first millennium of the Third Age, the power of the South Kingdom of Gondor grew, despite constant conflicts on its borders and the Easterling invasion of the fifth and sixth centuries. By the ninth century, Gondor had built a powerful navy to add to the military might of its army. By the eleventh century, Gondor had reached the height of its power, pushing back the Easterlings to the Sea of Rhûn, making Umbar a fortress of Gondor and subjugating the people of Harad.

Although the North Kingdom of Arnor never expanded its boundaries beyond Eriador, it prospered well enough until the ninth century. At that time internal disputes resulted in its division into three independent states, and these eventually fell to quarrelling among themselves.

The Riders of Rohan
allied with the Dúnedain.

THE CURSE OF SAURON

By the twelfth century, the spirit of Sauron had secretly returned to Middle-earth in the form of a single eye wreathed in flame. He found refuge in southern Mirkwood in the fortress of Dol Guldur. From this time onward, the forces of darkness grew steadily stronger throughout the lands of Middle-earth.

From the thirteenth century forward, Arnor was steadily diminished by a combination of natural disasters and internal strife. However, the greatest of its curses was Sauron's chief servant, the Lord of the Ringwraiths, who became the Witch-king of Angmar and maintained a state of war for over five centuries against Arnor's kings. Finally, in 1974, the Witch-king stormed the last Arnorian stronghold of Fornost, and Arnor ceased to exist as a kingdom. After the death of Arnor's twenty-third King, the royal bloodline was continued by the tribal Chieftains of the Dúnedain.

The decline of the South Kingdom of Arnor through the second millennium of the Third Age was attributed to three great curses. The first was the Kinstrife of the fifteenth century. This was a bloody civil war that resulted in thousands of deaths, the destruction of cities, the loss of most of Gondor's navy, and the end of its control of Umbar and Harad.

The second curse was the Great Plague of 1636, which Sauron loosed upon Gondor and Arnor. From this evil the Dúnedain never really recovered, for so many died at that time that parts of their realm remained empty forever after. The third curse was the Wainrider Invasions of the nineteenth and twentieth centuries. These invasions by a confederacy of well-armed Easterling peoples lasted for almost one hundred years. Although the Easterlings were finally driven back and defeated, they critically weakened the already diminished power of Gondor.

✳

Following page:
The Easterling Invasions.

*

The Witch-king of Angmar maintained a
state of war against Arnor's kings.

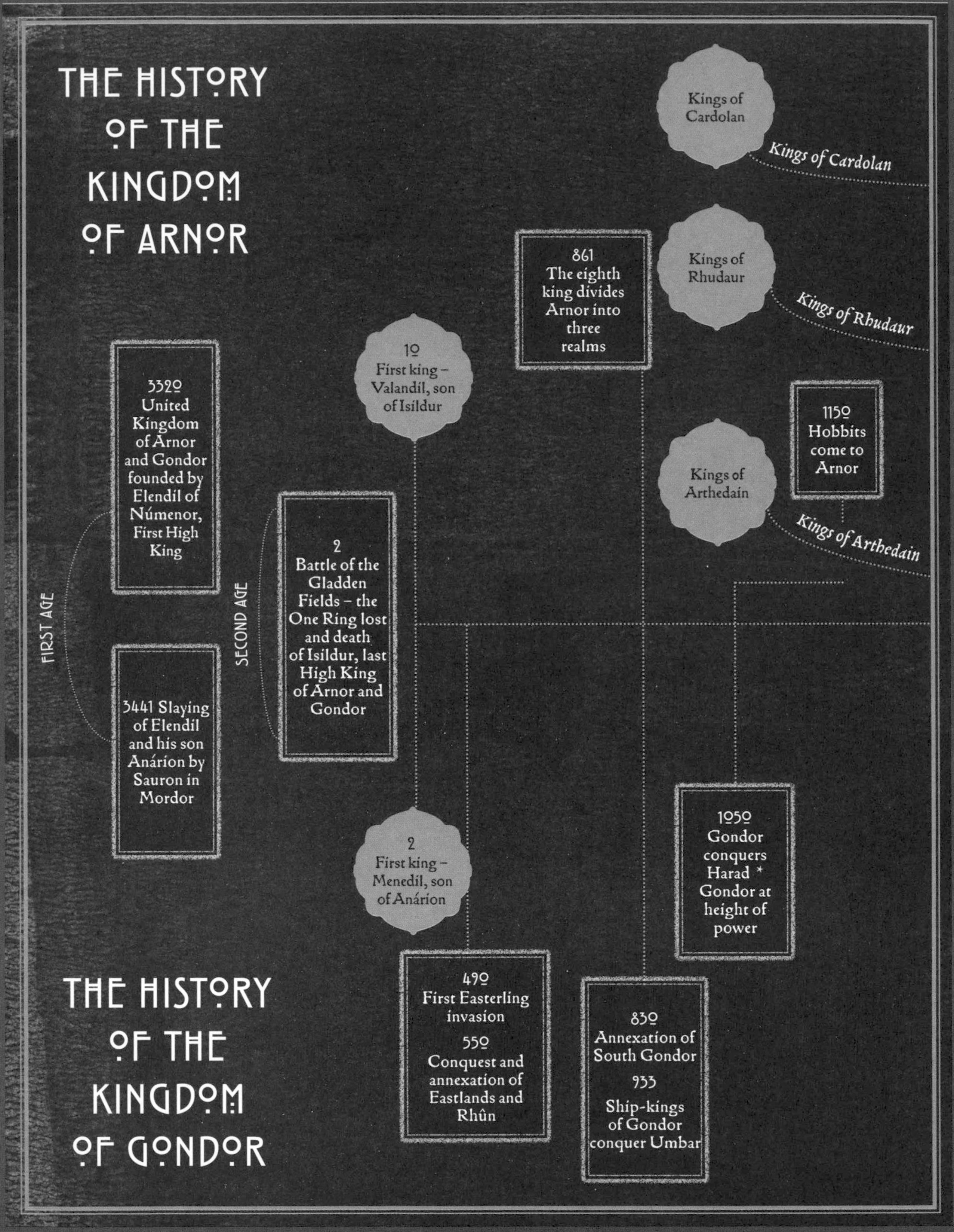

THE HISTORY OF THE KINGDOM OF ARNOR

Kings of Cardolan

Kings of Cardolan

861
The eighth king divides Arnor into three realms

Kings of Rhudaur

Kings of Rhudaur

1⍛
First king – Valandil, son of Isildur

1150
Hobbits come to Arnor

Kings of Arthedain

Kings of Arthedain

FIRST AGE

3320
United Kingdom of Arnor and Gondor founded by Elendil of Númenor, First High King

SECOND AGE

2
Battle of the Gladden Fields – the One Ring lost and death of Isildur, last High King of Arnor and Gondor

3441 Slaying of Elendil and his son Anárion by Sauron in Mordor

1050
Gondor conquers Harad * Gondor at height of power

2
First king – Menedil, son of Anárion

THE HISTORY OF THE KINGDOM OF GONDOR

490
First Easterling invasion

550
Conquest and annexation of Eastlands and Rhûn

830
Annexation of South Gondor

933
Ship-kings of Gondor conquer Umbar

1320 Line of kings fails

1409 Cardolan overrun ∗ Survivors take refuge in Barrow Downs ∗ Great Plague extinguishes last of Cardolanians

1300
Line of kings fails ∗ Hillmen usurp kingdom ∗ Hillmen become allies and eventual slaves of the Witch-king

1975
Realm of Hillmen of Rhudaur extinguished with Angmar

2911
Fell Winter ∗ Wolf raids

2912
Great Floods

2933
Aragorn II becomes sixteenth and last chieftain

1300
Witch-king in Angmar

1356
Defence of Tower of Weathertop from Hillmen

1409
Witch-king of Angmar invades Arnor ∗ Weathertop destroyed

1636
Great Plague

1974/5
Fornost falls to Witch-king ∗ End of Kingdom of Arnor ∗ Battle of Fornost ∗ Witch-king defeated ∗ End of Angmar ∗ Last king of Arnor drowned ∗ Line of Chieftains of Dúnedain begins Watchful Peace

2480
Orcs raid Eriador

2747
Orc raids ∗ Battle of Greenfields in the Shire

2758
Corsair and Orc raids ∗ Long Winter

1432
Civil war in Gondor

1437
Siege of Osgiliath

1448
Umbar seized by Corsairs

1540
War with Harad

1856
Wainrider invasion and conquest of Rhovanion

1899
Wainriders expelled

1944
Battle of Camp

2475
Witch-king destroys Osgiliath

2510
Balchoth Invasion ∗ Battle of Field of Celebrant

2885
Border wars with Harad

2901 Uruk raids on Ithilien

2984
Denethor II begins rule – 26th and last Ruling Steward

2940
Battle of the Five Armies

2942
Sauron in Mordor

1634
Corsairs devastate Pelargir

1636
Great Plague

2002
Witch-king seizes Minas Ithil

2050
Last King of Gondor slain ∗ Line of Ruling Stewards begins

2758
Easterling, Southron, Corsair and Dunlending invasion ∗ Long Winter

3019 War of the Ring ∗ Crowning of Elessar

THE MIGRATION
OF THE HOBBITS

Nothing is known of the Halfling people, who became known as the Hobbits, before 1050 of the Third Age. These were a burrowing, hole-dwelling people said to be related to Men, yet they were smaller than Dwarves, and the span of their lives was about a hundred years. Their first histories tell us they lived in the Northern Vales of Anduin between the Misty Mountains and Greenwood the Great. In the centuries that followed, they migrated westward and lived peacefully with Elves and Men in the land of Eriador.

All Hobbits measured between two and four feet in height, were long-fingered, possessed of a well-fed countenance, and had curly hair on peculiar shoeless, oversized feet. It is said that Hobbits were of three strains: Harfoots, Fallohides and Stoors. The Harfoots were the smallest and the most numerous, with nut-brown skin and hair. The Fallohides were taller and thinner, fair-haired and the least numerous, while the Stoors were the largest, bulkiest and most Mannish of the strains, and to the amazement of their kin, some could actually grow beards and chose to wear shoes. The Hobbits of Eriador primarily lived in the Mannish lands near the town of Bree until the year 1601. This was Year 1 in the Hobbit calendar of Shire Reckoning, when the greater part of the race marched westward again to the fertile lands beyond the Brandywine River. There, after this great migration, they settled down in the Shire, the land that was recognized always thereafter as the homeland of the Hobbits.

✳

Stoor, Fallohide and Harfoot Hobbits.

✳

The Hobbits marched westward beyond
the Brandywine River.

*

Azog the Uruk exults over the
body of a fallen dwarf.

THE BATTLE OF AZANULBIZAR

The final battle in the War of the Dwarves and the Orcs took place in Dimrill Dale, before the eastern gates of Moria. The Dwarves triumphed, but they also took heavy losses, including the death of Fundin, the father of Balin and Dwalin, who were to be among the Company of Adventurers that later journeyed to Lonely Mountain, and Náin, the father of Dáin Ironfoot. In this battle, Thorin Oakenshield gained his reputation as a great warrior by seizing a mighty oak branch as a weapon after being disarmed by Orcs. However, it was Dáin who finally slew the Orc chieftain Azog, avenging his fallen father.

✳

The Dwarves triumphed in the battle.

THE QUEST OF LONELY MOUNTAIN

*

Thorin and company approach Hobbiton.

THE QUEST
OF EREBOR

THE COMPANY OF ADVENTURERS

In the year 2941 of the Third Age of the Sun a Company of Adventurers entered the quiet lands of the Shire and disturbed the peace of that place. This Dwarf company of Thorin Oakenshield and Gandalf the Wizard were set on the Quest of Lonely Mountain. They had come to compel the Hobbit Bilbo Baggins to join them on their Quest. Thus the Hobbits of the Shire first became enmeshed in the affairs of greater nations in the world. For though the Shire was a peaceful land, it was like an oasis in a desert of war and strife. In the land of Mordor an evil power was growing that sought to crush all the good forces of the world.

Of the affairs of the world, the Hobbits knew very little, nor did they suspect the great part they were destined to play in the histories of Middle-earth. But all had its beginning in the coming of the Adventurers to the Shire and the desire of Thorin Oakenshield to wrest the inheritance of his people from Smaug, Dragon of Lonely Mountain.

GOLLUM AND THE GOBLIN CAVES

Among the first great challenges in Bilbo Baggins' quest was his descent into the Goblin caves wherein he escaped a Goblin attack, only to discover an even greater danger in the form of the cannibalistic creature known as Sméagol, or Gollum. In the deepest cavern by a dismal lake, Bilbo became entangled in a deadly riddle game, but also discovered a mysterious gold ring that had the power to make its wearer invisible. This ring eventually proved to be the long lost One Ring of Power that was once forged by Sauron the Ring Lord. It was a ring that carried with it a great curse of corruption, and as the Wizard Gandalf would learn many years later, it would be the spur to an even greater adventure and quest.

*

Gollum lived in a dark cave under the
Misty Mountains.

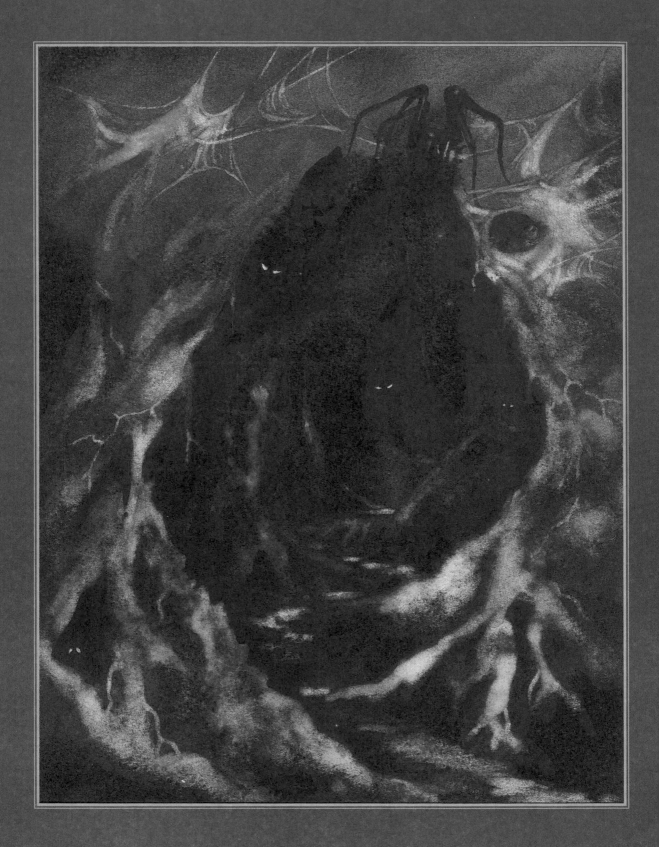

THE FOREST OF MIRKWOOD

The largest forest in Middle-earth was Greenwood the Great, where Thranduil made the Woodland Realm of the Silvan Elves. In the year 1050 of the Third Age a dark power had entered Greenwood. Great Spiders, Orcs, Wolves and evil spirits had haunted the forest and, though the Silvan Elves had not been driven from their realm, they had not been able to halt the spreading darkness. Thereafter Greenwood was called Mirkwood and few dared to travel along its dark paths.

Mirkwood was among the greatest obstacles standing before the company of Thorin Oakenshield on the road to Lonely Mountain.

SMAUG THE GOLDEN

When Bilbo Baggins and the Company of Dwarves finally reached Lonely Mountain of Erebor, they discovered the treasure of the King under the Mountain in the possession of the greatest dragon of the Third Age. Known as Smaug the Golden, this huge golden-red fire drake had bat-like wings and a coat of impenetrable iron scales. However, his one vulnerable part, his belly, was protected by a waistcoat of gems that had become embedded there from centuries of lying on jewelled treasure hoards. Although his beginnings are obscure, in the year 2770 of the Third Age, Smaug burned and sacked the city of Dale before entering the Dwarf Kingdom under the Mountain, where he slaughtered or drove out the Dwarves. For two centuries he lay on his hoard within Erebor. Then in 2941, his slumbers were disturbed by the Hobbit Bilbo Baggins and Thorin and Company.

Mirkwood was home to
many dreadful creatures.

Smaug lay for many years on his hoard.

THE DESTRUCTION OF LAKE-TOWN

The Lake Men of Esgaroth became complacent as they dwelt in peace in their town that stood above the water on stilts. It had been so long since Smaug had left Lonely Mountain that many people scoffed at the idea that he would ever return to attack them. However, Bilbo's theft of a cup from his hoard aroused the dragon to fury. He smashed the hiding place of the Dwarves high on the flank of Lonely Mountain, then sped above the ruins of Dale, towards Lake-town. Many of the townspeople believed the dragon's fire was the King under the Mountain forging gold. But it was not so, and their wooden town could muster little defence against the fires of an enraged dragon.

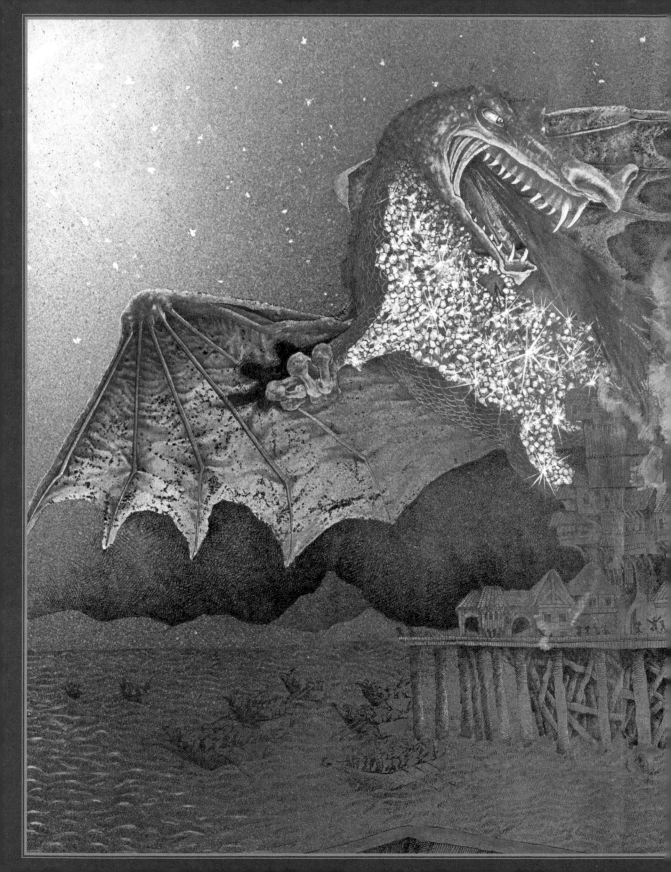

Once awakened, the Dragon of Erebor rose up in fiery
wrath against the Lake Men of Esgaroth.

The Battle of the Five Armies claimed the
lives of many Elves, Dwarves and Orcs.

THE BATTLE
OF THE FIVE ARMIES

The death of Smaug, the Dragon of Lonely Mountain, freed the treasures of the dragon's hoard from its guardian. The Dwarves of Thorin Oakenshield were soon joined by an army of Men from Lake-town, the army of the Elf-king of Mirkwood and an army of Dwarves from the Iron Hills. Yet another army, greater in number than the other four together, spilled into the valley under Lonely Mountain. It was led by a vast number of heinous Orcs from the Misty Mountains and they, too, came to claim the dragon's wealth. Orcs by the thousand, wolves and Wolf-riders, and clouds of blood-sucking bats fell on the gathered armies.

THE EAGLES
IN THE BATTLE

The Great Eagles of the Misty Mountains joined in against the legions of Orcs in the Battle of the Five Armies. These Eagles were of such size that they were capable of carrying Men, Dwarves and Hobbits aloft in their flight. They were the noble descendants of the Eagles of Beleriand, who in the First Age fought in the War of Wrath against the winged fire dragons of Morgoth. During the Quest of Lonely Mountain, Great Eagles inhabited the eastern slopes of the Misty Mountains, near the High Pass leading from Rivendell and not far from Goblin-town. There, they harried the Goblins and their allies, and rescued the Dwarves of the Company of Adventurers from a band of Goblins and Wargs. Later they would become allies and rescuers of members of the Fellowship of the Ring at critical moments of the quest.

The Battle of the Five Armies was
a bloody and chaotic affair.

THE QUEST OF
THE RING

THE RINGS OF POWER IN THE SECOND AND THIRD AGES

1500 *Rings of Power forged by Sauron and Elven-smiths of Eregion (Three Elf Rings, Seven Dwarf Rings, Nine Rings for Men)*

1603 *War of Sauron and Elves. Three Elf Rings hidden (Gil-galad in Lindon, Círdan in Grey Havens, Galadriel in Lothlórien)*

1600 *Sauron forges One Ring in Fires of Mount Doom*

2251 *Ringwraiths, slaves of the Nine Rings, come to serve Sauron*

3430 *Last Alliance of Elves and Men formed*

3441 *One Ring cut from Sauron's hand. Mordor falls. Sauron and Ringwraiths vanish*

1 *Gil-Galad's Elf-ring goes with Elrond to Rivendell*

2 *Battle of Gladden Fields. One Ring lost in Anduin River*

1000 *Sauron in Mirkwood, secretly gathers Rings*

1050 *Wizards come to Middle-earth. Círdan gives Elf-ring to Gandalf*

1200 *Ringwraiths appear in north*

1300 *Lord of Ringwraiths becomes Witch-king of Angmar*

1975 *Angmar destroyed*

1980 *Ringwraiths dwelling in Mordor*

2002 *Witch-king begins rule in Minas Morgul*

2470 *Gollum takes One Ring into Misty Mountains*

2463 *One Ring found by Déagol in the Anduin*

2845 *Sauron seizes last of the Seven Dwarf Rings*

2941 *Bilbo Baggins finds One Ring in the Misty Mountains*

3001 *Bilbo Baggins gives One Ring to Frodo Baggins*

3018 *Fellowship of the Ring formed*

3021 *The War of the Ring begins. One Ring destroyed. Mordor falls. Sauron and Ringwraiths vanish forever*

3021 *Keepers of the Elf Rings sail to Undying Lands*

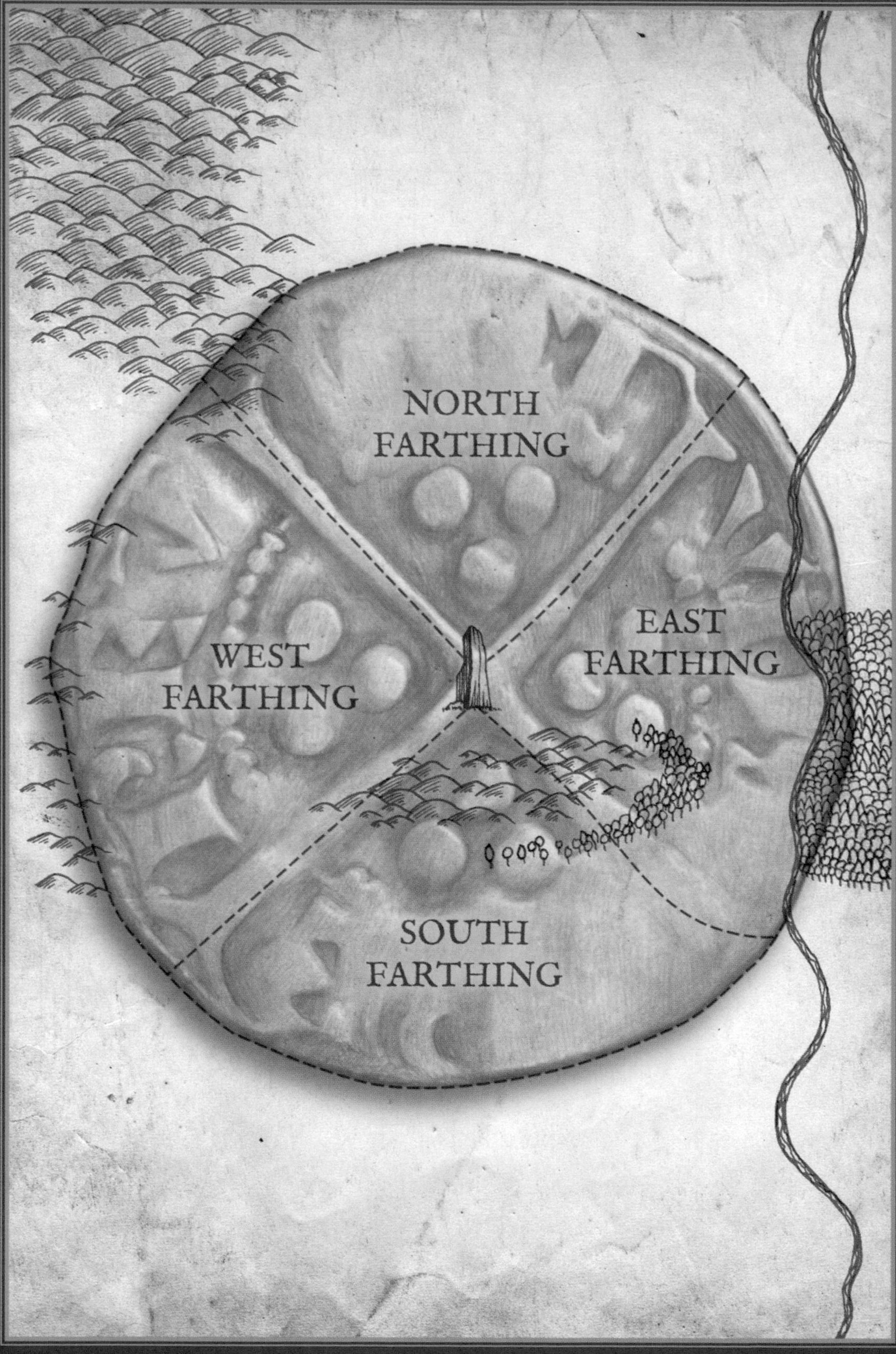

NORTH
FARTHING

EAST
FARTHING

WEST
FARTHING

SOUTH
FARTHING

THE SHIRE

The green and pleasant lands of the Shire had been the homeland of the Hobbits since the seventeenth century of the Third Age of the Sun. Here lived Bilbo Baggins, who joined the Quest of Lonely Mountain and on that adventure acquired a magic Ring. This chance discovery drew Bilbo, his heir Frodo Baggins and all the Hobbits of the Shire into the greatest drama of that Age. So it was that the meekest and least of all peoples came to hold the fate of all the world in their hands.

✳

**The Shire was situated in the peaceful
north-west of Middle-earth.**

The Barrow-downs were haunted by evil
spirits known as Barrow-wights.

THE BARROW-DOWNS

To the east of the Shire and the Old Forest lay the Barrow-downs, an ancient burial ground. There were no trees or water on these downlands, only grass covering dome-shaped hills that were ringed and crowned with stone monoliths. Considered by many during the Third Age to be the most ancient burial ground of Men on Middle-earth, these barrow graves of royal ancestors were revered by the Dúnedain of Arnor. By the time of the Ring Quest, these burial chambers were haunted by evil spirits known as Barrow-wights, who had their origin in the Witch-king's realm of Angmar. Passing through this haunted land, the Ringbearer, Frodo Baggins, was drawn into a burial vault and succumbed to the hypnotic spell of these undead phantoms.

THE FORD OF BRUINEN

The Ford of Bruinen was an enchanted river crossing guarded by Elvish powers. For in crossing the river at this ford, one entered the hidden refuge of Imladris. Also known as Rivendell, this was the domain of Elrond Half-elven, who possessed one of the Three Rings of the Elves. It was by the enchantment of Elrond's ring that the Ford was guarded and the refuge of Rivendell remained hidden from the world. During the Quest of Lonely Mountain, after their passage though the Trollshaws, Thorin and Company were permitted to cross the Ford and enter Rivendell. While in the Quest of the Ring, it was at the Ford of Bruinen that Frodo Baggins was attacked by the Nine Black Riders, those terrible undead servants of Sauron also known as the Ringwraiths.

Following page: The river rose in wrath against the Black Riders.

THE LAST HOMELY HOUSE EAST OF THE SEA

In the wake of the War of Sauron and the Elves during the Second Age, Master Elrond Half-elven led the surviving Elven-smiths of Eriador to the refuge of Rivendell in the steep, hidden valley of Imladris at the foot of the Misty Mountains. Here was hidden the House of Elrond. Known as the 'Last Homely House East of the Sea', it was a house of wisdom and great learning, and served as a refuge for all Elves and Men of goodwill. It was here that Bilbo Baggins found peace after his adventures, and it was here that Frodo Baggins found refuge after the attack of the Ringwraiths at the Ford. It was also in Rivendell where the Fellowship of the Ring was formed, and the Quest of the Ring was planned. After the War of the Ring, Elrond left Rivendell for the Undying Lands, and although many of the other Elves remained for a time, the refuge was finally abandoned in the Fourth Age when the last Elven ship departed from the Grey Havens.

The Last Homely House
nestled in its valley.

THE MINES
OF MORIA

Most ancient and famous of all the Dwarf kingdoms was that realm originally called Khazad-dûm, the ancestral home of Durin the Deathless, the first of the seven Fathers of the Dwarves. Through five Ages of Stars and three Ages of the Sun the Dwarves of Khazad-dûm were prosperous and strong. In the Second Age of the Sun, these were the Dwarves who had a long friendship with the Gwaith-i-Mírdain, the Elven-smiths of Eregion, who forged the Rings of Power. But in the Accursed Years of Sauron's dominion in the Second Age, the Dwarves had closed their great doors to the world. At this time, the mansion was renamed Moria, the 'dark chasm'.

Yet still the Dwarves quarried and worked the forges beneath the Misty Mountains until 1980 of the Third Age of the Sun. In that year the Dwarves delved too deep beneath Mount Barazinbar, and an entombed Balrog was released within the halls of Moria. So terrible was the Balrog's strength and wrath that the Dwarves were either slain or driven from their kingdom.

When the Fellowship of the Ring entered Moria it was therefore a chasm of darkness that had long been abandoned by Dwarves. Its treasures had been stripped by Orkish hordes and through its barren corridors there still walked the Balrog and many bands of Orcs and Trolls.

✳

By the Third Age, Khazad-dûm had become the
dark and forbidding Mines of Moria.

Zirak-zigil, one of the cruel peaks
of the Misty Mountains.

ZIRAK-ZIGIL
AND DURIN'S TOWER

Among the many snowy peaks in the Misty Mountains stands Zirak-zigil, one of the three great mountains that tower over the Dwarf kingdom of Moria. It was also known as Silvertine by Men, and Celebdil by the Elves. The other two peaks of Moria were named Fanuidhol and Caradhras by the Elves, and were commonly called Cloudyhead and Redhorn. Within the pinnacle of Zirak-zigil – at the top of the winding Endless Stair – was a lookout chamber called Durin's Tower. At the end of the Third Age the Wizard Gandalf did battle with the Balrog of Moria. In this Battle of the Peak, the Endless Stair and Durin's Tower were destroyed.

THE GOLDEN FOREST
OF LOTHLÓRIEN

The fairest Elf-kingdom remaining on Middle-earth in the Third Age was Lothlórien, where the Noldor lady Galadriel and the Sindar lord Celeborn ruled. In this wooded realm the tallest and fairest trees of Middle-earth grew, and some part of the brilliance of the Elf-kingdoms of ancient times seemed to glow.

At the very heart of Lothlórien was the hill of Cerin Amroth, where the house of the Elf-king Amroth once stood. It was said to be a fair and enchanted place where the Elf-flowers Elanor and Niphredil constantly bloomed. Here Arwen, daughter of Elrond Half-elven, and Aragorn, son of Arathorn, pledged their love; and to this hill Arwen returned in the Fourth Age to seek her final place of rest.

Into the magical realm of Lothlórien came the Fellowship of the Ring, fleeing the servants of Sauron, and there among these Elves, the Galadhrim, they found shelter and rest.

The Galadhrim were wise in the ways of the forest and they lived almost invisibly on high platforms in the trees. Lothlórien was also protected by the power of Galadriel and the Elf Ring Nenya, the Ring of Adamant.

The Golden Forest
of Lothlórien.

ARGONATH,
THE GATES OF GONDOR

The Argonath was a pair of massive sculptures cut into the towering cliffs on either side of the river gorge that fed into a lake above the great fall of Rauros on the Anduin River. Argonath means the 'royal stones', but they were also known as the Pillars of the Kings or the Gates of Gondor because the images in stone were of Isildur and Anárion, the first kings of Gondor. These massive figures were carved in the living rock in the year 1340 of the Third Age to mark the northern limit of the kingdom of Gondor. And it was by way of the river and through these gates that Frodo the Ringbearer and the Fellowship of the Ring passed on their quest.

THE RAUROS FALLS

The most spectacular waterfall on Middle-earth in the Third Age was the Rauros Falls on the Great River Anduin on the northern border of Gondor. The name Rauros means 'roaring foam' and accurately described the high waterfall as it fell in a shimmering golden haze from the long lake of Nen Hithoel on the heights of Emyn Muil to the marshlands far below. The falls were unnavigable, but a portage route called the North Stair had been cut in the cliffs as a means of bypassing them. During the Quest of the Ring, the funeral boat of Boromir was sent over the Rauros Falls.

The Pillars of the Kings towered
over the River Anduin.

*

The boat bearing Boromir passed
unharmed over the Falls of Rauros.

SARUMAN

Curumo, one of the Maiar of Aulë, was the leader of the Istari – the five wizards sent from the Undying Lands to aid the people of Middle-earth. Known as Saruman the White to Men, he was wise and learned, but became so proud that he sought to find the One Ring and wield it himself. Renaming himself Saruman of Many Colours, he commanded armies of Orcs and Men from his stronghold of Isengard.

Saruman the White was at first
the leader of the Istari.

THE
WAR
OF THE
RING

The Golden Hall of the Rohirrim was
a place of feasting and warmth.

THE GOLDEN HALL
OF THE ROHIRRIM

The greatest allies of the Dúnedain in the Third Age were the Rohirrim. These were the finest horsemen of Middle-earth and from Meduseld, the Golden Hall, their kings had ruled Rohan for five hundred years. At the outbreak of the War of the Ring, however, the Rohirrim withheld their aid from the Dúnedain because their king was under the vile influence of the rebel Wizard Saruman. But Gandalf and three others of the Fellowship of the Ring came to the Golden Hall, and because of these emissaries the knights of Rohan cast off their fear. Honouring their old alliance with the Dúnedain of Gondor, the Rohirrim bravely entered the War of the Ring.

The Battle of the Hornburg was one of the
most decisive in the War of the Ring.

King Théoden rode into battle
with the Rohirrim.

THE BATTLE OF
THE HORNBURG

Before the Rohirrim could support their allies – the Men of Gondor – in the War of the Ring against the Dark Lord of Mordor, they discovered they must first deal with an enemy that had arisen within their own lands. For the army of the rebel Wizard Saruman, which comprised a multitude of Uruk-hai, Orcs, Half-orcs and fierce Dunlendings, had advanced out of Isengard and had come wrathfully on the Horsemen of Rohan. At great cost, the army of Isengard drove the Rohirrim before them, until the Horsemen were forced to seek refuge in the ancient citadel in Helm's Deep called the Hornburg. Here, three of the Ring Fellowship – Aragorn, the Dwarf Gimli and the Elf-prince Legolas – joined the Rohirrim.

At Hornburg, one of the great battles in the War of the Ring was fought as the enemy stormed the earthwork defences and the high walls, and battered the great gate of the ancient citadel.

THE WALLS
OF ISENGARD

In the War of the Ring, it seemed that the evil allies of Sauron the Ring Lord arose everywhere out of the dark lands. One such mighty ally was the rebel Wizard Saruman who held the tower and citadel of Isengard. Once thought to be a friend of the Men of Gondor and Rohan and therefore granted the keys to Isengard, Saruman later became seduced by the Ring Lord and was drawn into league with him. Thereafter Saruman surrounded himself with Orcs, Uruk-hai, Dunlendings and Half-orcs.

Other beings unexpectedly came into the War because they had been harmed by the servants of Saruman, who had burned and laid waste the forests about Isengard. The mighty giants called Ents came against Saruman. Half-Men, half-trees, these ancient guardians of the forests were the tallest and strongest race on Middle-earth. Rank upon rank of these vengeful giants attacked the very walls of Isengard.

Isengard could not withstand
the wrath of the Ents.

THE
JOURNEY
OF THE
RING-BEARER

THE DEAD MARSHES

Between the Falls of Rauros on the River Anduin and the mountains of Mordor was the vast fenland called the Dead Marshes. On this foul, trackless wasteland few ever dared to travel, for not only were the Marshes pathless and the waters stagnant and poisoned, but they were also haunted by the phantoms of dead Men, Elves and Orcs. Yet, to achieve his Quest, Frodo the Ringbearer and his companion had to cross the Marshes, so they forced the creature called Gollum to guide them through this vile land.

Gollum leads Frodo and Sam through the
foul-smelling maze of the marshes.

*

Henneth Annun
was a glorious sight.

THE WINDOW
OF THE SUNSET

Henneth Annun, or the 'Window of the Sunset', was a cavern refuge of the Rangers of Ithilien that was hidden behind the curtain of a spectacular waterfall in the north of Ithilien. Its waters flowed into the River Anduin near the Field of Cormallen and just south of Cair Andros. It was a natural cave formation that was further excavated by Turin of Gondor in 2901 of the Third Age. During the War of the Ring it was often used by Faramir and his Rangers. The Ringbearer, Frodo Baggins, was given shelter in this refuge during the Quest of the Ring.

SHELOB
THE GREAT

In the mountains of Mordor there was one little-used pass called Cirith Ungol. Few ever attempted to enter Mordor this way, for the guardian of the pass was Shelob the Great, last ancient daughter of Ungoliant, the Great Spider that had destroyed the Trees of the Valar.

Dangerous as this pass was, the Ringbearer and his companion dared it, for this was their only chance of entry into Mordor. By the treachery of Gollum and the strength of Shelob, the Ringbearer was struck down and brought near death until his servant, Samwise Gamgee, valiantly leapt to his defence.

Shelob was daunted by the light from
the Phial of Galadriel.

THE MOUNTAINS OF MORDOR

After their narrow escape from Shelob the Great and the Orcs of the Tower of Cirith Ungol, the Hobbits attempted to climb the Morgai – the 'Black Fence' – an eastern ridge in the Ephel Dúath, the 'Mountains of the Shadows', that formed the inner wall of Mordor's western mountains. The edge of the ridge was notched and jagged with fang-like crags, and was separated from the Ephel Dúath by a trough, in which a road lead to the north. From the heights of the Morgai, the two Hobbits looked down onto the dismal barren plateau of Gorgoroth, and beyond; eastward they could spy where their quest must end in the volcanic fires of Mount Doom.

The dreadful tower of Barad-dûr
loomed over Mordor.

Minas Tirith was an awesome sight.

MINAS TIRITH

Minas Tirith, meaning 'The Tower of Guard' in Sindarin, was the capital of Gondor in the second half of the Third Age, after the city of Osgiliath fell into ruin. It was originally named Minas Anor, Sindarin for 'Tower of the Setting Sun'.

The city was built on seven levels, all except the first of them divided by a huge spur of rock jutting from the mountains behind. The seventh level, at the same height as the top of the spur, contained the Citadel of Gondor with the 300-foot Tower of Ecthelion rising from its centre. In the courtyard in front of the tower grew the White Tree, the symbol of Gondor. In a secret chamber at the top of the tower, the Stewards of Gondor kept the Seeing Stone of Minas Anor.

Minas Tirith was surrounded by the Pelennor Fields, which were peaceful farmland until the great Battle of the Pelennor Fields was fought there at the climax of the War of the Ring.

DUNHARROW AND THE DWIMORBERG

Among the most ancient fortresses upon Middle-earth was Dunharrow in Rohan. This refuge could only be approached by a switchback road up the steep cliffs of the mountains. It was a monumental piece of engineering. The road reached a wall of rock at the top through which a gap was cut, and an incline led on to the Hold of Dunharrow. This was a high, broad alpine meadow on which thousands could encamp themselves in times of war. Upon this was a great corridor of unshaped, black standing stones which led straight to the Dwimorberg, the 'Haunted Mountain', and a black wall of stone pierced by the 'Dark Door', a massive archway also known as the 'Gate of the Dead'. This led to a secret glen that was haunted by the spirits of the dead who prevented living men from crossing to the far side of the White Mountains by means of this abandoned pass. During the War of the Ring, it was through these Paths of the Dead that Aragorn the future king rode. As heir to the Dúnedain kingdoms, he recruited and commanded a ghostly army of these Dead Men of Dunharrow.

Following pages: The entrance to
Dunharrow led down into darkness.

MINAS MORGUL

In the year 2002 of the Third Age, the fortress-city of Minas Ithil, the 'Tower of the Moon', was captured after a two-year siege by the forces of the Nazgûl Witch-king, who renamed it Minas Morgul, the 'Tower of the Wraiths'. It was also called the Tower of Sorcery and the Dead City. Similar in structure to its great rival, Minas Tirith, it became a haunted and wicked place that shone in the night with a ghostly light. By some magical power or fiendish machinery, the upper rooms of its great tower revolved slowly in constant vigilance. For over a thousand years, Minas Morgul was ruled by the terror of the Ringwraiths, and this resulted in the almost total ruin and depopulation of the fief of Ithilien. In the year 2050 the Witch-king of Morgul slew Eärnur, the last king of Gondor. In 2475 Osgiliath was sacked including its stone bridge, which was broken by the Witch-king's army of giant Orcs known as Uruk-hai. During the War of the Ring, Minas Morgul played a key role in Sauron's strategies. The forces out of Morgul were the first to move directly against Gondor and overrun Osgiliath.

✳

Following pages: Gandalf and the
Witch-king ride under the same moon.

The once-fair Minas Ithil became the
black tower of Minas Morgul.

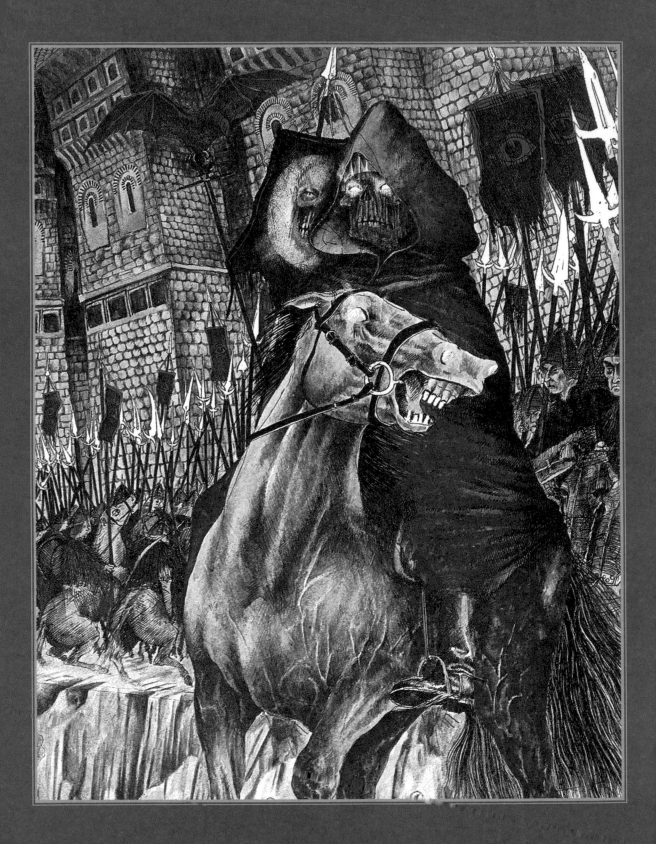

THE WITCH-KING

The Witch-king was originally a sorcerer king of the Second Age who was given the first of the Nine Rings of Mortal Men by Sauron the Ring Lord. The Witch-king became the Lord of the Nazgûl Ringwraiths. In 1300 of the Third Age, he rose up in the form of the Witch-king of Angmar, and laid waste to the North-kingdom of the Dúnedain. In the second millennium of the Third Age, he began his attacks on the South-kingdom. As the Witch-king of Morgul, he fought and harried the men of Gondor for a thousand years. He led a mighty army to the Battle of the Pelennor Fields, the decisive conflict of the War of the Ring.

THE PELENNOR FIELDS

The greatest battle of the War of the Ring was fought on Pelennor Fields before the White Tower of Gondor, which was besieged by the army of the Witch-king of Morgul. Haradrim cavalry and infantry in scarlet and gold marched into battle with elephantine Mûmakil, Variags of Khand and axe-bearing Easterlings. Orcs, Uruk-hai, Olog-hai, Trolls and Half-orcs out of Mordor joined this vast host. Ranged against them were the Captains of the Outlands from Dol Amroth, Lossarnach, Anfalas, Morthond, Ethir and Pinnath Gelin. This army of Gondor was driven back from Osgiliath and Rammas Echor to seek shelter within the citadel of Minas Tirith. For two days and two nights the battle raged. Siege towers, catapults and great arms battered the walls and rained fire and stones on the Men of Gondor. All seemed lost; darkness covered the land, the Morgul hordes swarmed over the Field, and the Witch-king shattered the great gates of the city. Then, unexpectedly, the Rohirrim allies of Gondor rode into the Field to join the fray.

The Witch-king of Morgul.

The enemy forces at the Battle of
Pelennor Fields included Mûmakil.

ÉOWYN AND
THE WITCH-KING

The Witch-king believed his moment of ultimate victory had come when he led his vast Morgul army and his Haradrim allies into the Battle of Pelennor Fields. Protected by the prophecy that he could not be slain by the hand of a man, the Witch-king discovered in the midst of the din of battle that the opponent before him was the Shield-maiden, Éowyn of Rohan. She dared to withstand the most terrible of the servants of Sauron and stood firm in the face of the wraith and his monstrous steed.

❊

The Witch-king
and the Shield-maiden.

THE BATTLE OF THE PELENNOR FIELDS

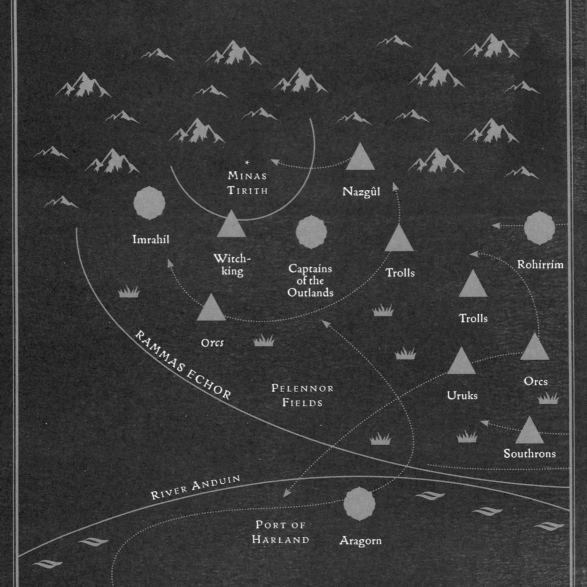

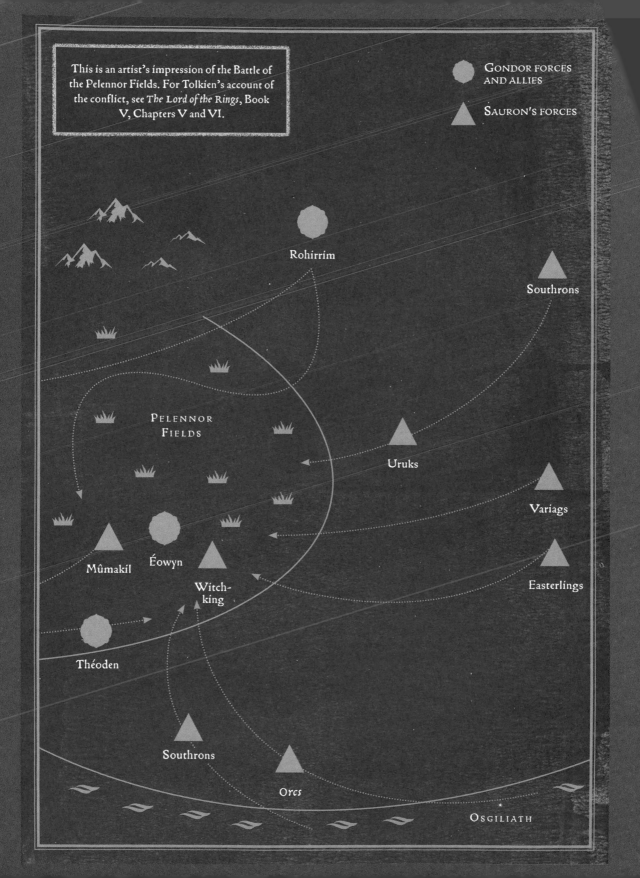

This is an artist's impression of the Battle of the Pelennor Fields. For Tolkien's account of the conflict, see *The Lord of the Rings*, Book V, Chapters V and VI.

GONDOR FORCES AND ALLIES

SAURON'S FORCES

Rohirrim

Southrons

PELENNOR FIELDS

Uruks

Variags

Mûmakil

Éowyn

Easterlings

Witch-king

Théoden

Southrons

Orcs

OSGILIATH

THE CRACKS OF DOOM

The immense volcanic mountain of Mordor, known as Mount Doom, was more properly called Orodruin, meaning 'mountain of blazing fire'. This was the fire and forge of Sauron who, within the Chambers of Fire and the fissures called the Cracks of Doom within its volcanic cone, made the One Ring in the year 1600 of the Second Age. The existence of the Cracks of Doom was critical to the War of the Ring, for only there could the One Ring be unmade and Sauron's power destroyed. In the year 3019, Frodo Baggins reached his destination on the edge of the Cracks of Doom, but in a moment of indecision, he hesitated and the One Ring was seized by Gollum.

THE DESTRUCTION OF MORDOR

For over five millennia, the 'black land' of Mordor was Sauron the Ring Lord's base of power in his quest for dominion over all Middle-earth. Mordor was defended on three sides by mountain ranges. Its central plateau of Gorgoroth was a vast dreary place of slag heaps and Orc pits always under a pall of smoke from the volcanic Mount Doom near its centre. Here, too, was Barad-dûr, Sauron's Dark Tower of Mordor. Another name for Mount Doom was Amon Amarth, the 'mountain of fate', as the fires in its volcanic heart rose at Sauron's command and in his absence fell and became dormant. At each return, the volcano erupted. As the Quest of the Ring ended – mirroring the fate of the Dark Lord – Amon Amarth burst forth in one last cataclysm that brought ruin to all of Mordor.

Following page:
The Ruin of Mordor.

Gollum falling.

THE FOURTH AGE

EARTH'S ATMOSPHERE

LINDON

REUNITED
KINGDOM

WEST SEA

HARAD

RHÛN

FAR HARAD

MIDDLE-
EARTH

HITHER
LANDS

EAST SEA

SUNLANDS

DARK LANDS

SOLAR SYSTEM

Years 37,063–40,000 (Historic Time)

THE FOURTH AGE OF THE SUN

When the last Elven ship finally reached the immortal shores during the Fourth Age, the Undying Lands vanished into another dimension, beyond human understanding. The globed world increasingly evolved into the mortal planet of Earth. The land-masses drifted towards the familiar shapes of our known world. And, as mythic time passed into recorded historic time, the Earth began to orbit the sun in the physical universe.

THE HIGH KING OF THE REUNITED KINGDOM

Aragorn son of Arathorn was also known as Elessar (meaning 'Elfstone'), the Dúnadan and heir of Isildur of Gondor. At the onset of the Quest of the Ring, Aragorn was the sixteenth Chieftain of the Dúnedain of the North, but was known more humbly as Strider the Ranger. As one of the Fellowship of the Ring, he played a major part in the battles at Hornburg, Pelennor Fields and the Black Gate of Mordor. After the end of the War of the Ring, he was crowned King Elessar Telcontar, the first High King of the Reunited Kingdom of Arnor and Gondor. He married the Elven princess Arwen Evenstar, and during the next century of his reign, Elessar extended his kingdom to most of the western lands of Middle-earth. Though he crushed many enemies in war, he made peace with the Easterlings and the Haradrim, and in the Fourth Age of the Sun, which was ordained the Age of the Dominion of Men, there was peace in the Westlands, and also for many years after that time because of the wisdom of Elessar and his heirs.

THE DEPARTURE OF THE RINGBEARERS

When the War of the Ring ended there was peace and prosperity in Middle-earth once again. At that time it was also ordained that the great Elvish powers should pass from Mortal Lands. So it was that Elrond, Galadriel and Gandalf, the keepers of the Three Elf Rings, and Bilbo and Frodo Baggins, two bearers of the Ruling Ring, came to the Grey Havens. In an Elven-ship, they sailed westwards to the Undying Lands.

The Ringbearers departed for
the West in an Elven-ship.

When the War of the Ring ended
there was peace and prosperity in
Middle-earth once again.

INDEX